The Holy Longing

Other books by

Connie Zweig

Nonfiction

To Be A Woman (Ed.)

Meeting the Shadow (Ed. with Jeremiah Abrams)

Romancing the Shadow (with Steve Wolf)

Fiction

A Moth to the Flame: The Life Story of Sufi Poet Rumi

The Holy Longing

✦

Spiritual Yearning and Its Shadow Side

Revised Edition

Connie Zweig, Ph.D.

iUniverse, Inc.
New York Bloomington Shanghai

The Holy Longing
Spiritual Yearning and Its Shadow Side

iUniverse books may be ordered through booksellers or by contacting:

iUniverse
1663 Liberty Drive
Bloomington, IN 47403
www.iuniverse.com
1-800-Authors (1-800-288-4677)

Because of the dynamic nature of the Internet, any Web addresses or links contained in this book may have changed since publication and may no longer be valid.

ISBN: 978-0-595-44910-1 (pbk)
ISBN: 978-0-595-89233-4 (ebk)

Printed in the United States of America

1. "The Holy Longing" by Goethe (translated by Robert Bly) was reprinted from *News of the Universe: Poems of Two-Fold Consciousness,* edited by Robert Bly, Sierra Club Books, San Francisco, 1980. Copyright 1980 Robert Bly. Used with permission.

2. An earlier version of Creativity as Practice appeared in *The Spirit of Writing,* ed. Mark Waldman, published by Tarcher/Putnam.

To Neil

who wears the face of the Beloved for me

As the deer pants after the water brooks, so pants my soul after thee, O God.

—Psalms 42:1

Could the longing for a god be a passion welling up from our darkest, instinctual nature, a passion unswayed by any outside influences, deeper and stronger perhaps than the love for a human person?

—C.G. Jung

When the Guest is being searched for, it is the intensity of the longing for the Guest that does all the work. Look at me, and you will see a slave of that intensity.

—Kabir (trans. Robert Bly)

Contents

Acknowledgments xiii

Prologue: My Longing for the Light: A Meditation on Up 1

Part I   *Before the Fall: A Guide for Faithful Believers*

CHAPTER 1   The Holy Longing 14

Awakening to holy longing 18

God longs for us as we long for god 22

The Inner Marriage: A story of holy longing in the Sufi poet Rumi 25

CHAPTER 2   Longing for God: The Hidden Object of Desire . 32

The Changing God Image: Involution or Down 34

The Changing God Image: Evolution or Up 41

The Inner Marriage: A Story of Holy Longing in the Hindu Master
Ramakrishna 45

CHAPTER 3   Longing for the Human Beloved: The Search for
Romantic Union 50

Beloved as parent: the psychology of love 53

Beloved as god: the archetypes of love 57

The inner marriage: A story of holy longing in the Sufi lovers Majnun and
Layla 60

CHAPTER 4   Longing for the Divine Human: The Search for
Spiritual Communion 66

Priest or teacher as parent: the psychology of spirituality 68

Priest or teacher as god: the archetypes of spirituality 76

Priest or teacher as divine human: the teacher/student relationship 83

The inner marriage: A story of holy longing in the Christian saint Catherine of Siena 84

Part II   After the Fall: A Guide for Disillusioned Believers

CHAPTER 5   Meeting Spiritual Shadow: Darkness on the Path 94

Encountering the spiritual Other: the breakdown of communion 98

The consequences of spiritual abuse 109

Uncovering patterns of abuse 112

Who is susceptible to spiritual abuse? 119

Meeting the shadow of addiction 124

Death and transcendence 126

Midlogue: My Longing for the Dark: A Meditation on Down 129

CHAPTER 6   Rekindling the Flame: Shadow-work for Spiritual Abuse and Disillusionment 133

Communal shadow-work 134

Separating from a teacher and imago dei 139

Reclaiming the light 141

Reclaiming independent thinking 142

Reclaiming authentic feeling 145

Reclaiming the body 147

Reclaiming action on our own behalf 149

Reclaiming images of the divine 151

Creativity as practice 159

Finding our spiritual myths 162

A New Epilogue: Through the Shadow to the Light 165

Acknowledgments

Writing a book is essentially a solitary task. But I wish to honor my psychological ancestors, whose work is my inspiration, especially Sigmund Freud, Carl Jung, James Hillman, and Ken Wilber. And I wish to thank the community of Pacifica Graduate Institute, especially my dissertation committee: Dr. Aaron Kipnis, Dr. Dianne Skafte, and Dr. Claire Douglas. That research formed the seed of this book.

Gratitude to the many people who have shared their tales of spiritual longing and disillusionment with me, as well as to those who have written their stories with honesty and authenticity, which I retell here.

To Candice Fuhrman, agent and friend, who shepherded this work into the world.

To Jeremy Tarcher, Joel Fotinos, and Mitch Horowitz, at Tarcher/Putnam, who published the original edition of this book.

To Steve Reicher, my first *imago amore*. I will not forget you.

To the teacher who lit the fire more than thirty years ago and to all my teachers since, who have helped to keep it burning.

To Joan Harrigan, whose profound wisdom and steadfast guidance relit the dying embers.

To my *satsang*: no words can suffice. You welcomed me home.

To friends and colleagues for reading the manuscript and spending precious time discussing these ideas with me: Tom Rautenberg, Demaris Wehr, Bryan Wittine, Naomi Lowinsky, Bob Forman, Aaron Kipnis, Marsha de la O, Jeff Utter, Tony Stern.

To my beloved giggle group—Neil, Janet Bachelor, Terry Crowe, Bruce Langhorn, Maureen Nathan, Linda Novack, Paula Perlman, Rhoda Pregerson, Linda Schreyer, Malcolm Schultz, Steve Wolf—for the best belly laughs during the decades of our friendship.

Prologue: My Longing for the Light: A Meditation on Up

As a meditation practitioner for nearly 40 years, I have been insane for the light. Like a moth diving into the flame, I sought to be consumed in the burning, cooked, turned to ash.

At times, on my knees, arms outstretched to the heavens, I beseeched my god. At other times, sitting still like a yogi for hours on end, my senses switched off, I turned an ear within to hear my god. Occasionally, for moments, the timbre of a celestial voice suggested itself; the horizon of another realm shimmered. But, at other times, disappointed and exhausted, I suffered the indifference of my god.

At age 19, I turned toward the East. The turn back did not begin until 12 years later. Today, in certain ways, I am still struggling to make the turn.

A student at UC Berkeley at the time, enjoying an intellectual, politically active, experimental lifestyle, I learned meditation for no holy reason or higher motivation but to date a man who would not get involved unless I learned the practice. I had no idea how this seemingly light-hearted decision would radically alter the course of my life.

After about a year of sitting, eyes closed and legs crossed, several internal changes had taken place: My chatterbox mind, usually highly active and alert, was quieting down. At bedtime, it was not full of obsessive or random thoughts, which kept me awake. My breathing, too, was quieter, softer and gentler, so that my body felt calm rather than agitated much of the time. Emotionally I felt more stable inside. Friends commented that I seemed less angry.

As my emotional turmoil subsided, I grew less engaged politically with "the enemy" out there and more engaged with the battleground within. I also grew less interested in saving the world through social activism and more interested in saving myself through the development of consciousness. Increasingly drawn to the meditative state, to the ocean of silence that pulled me away from complicated relationships and toward the simple goal of making that silence permanent—enlightenment—I began to long for god.

I signed up for a month-long retreat that involved meditating for many hours each day and listening to long lectures at night. Sitting in the hall that first morn-

1

ing with several thousand others, whose restless eagerness could not be detected in the stillness, I awaited the guru. I wanted to be calm, yet alert, open, yet unattached—in the correct state of mind for him. I wanted to please him already.

A door opened and a tall, stately man in saffron robes glided into the room. A bushy beard, just beginning to gray, covered his face. He folded his knees beneath him on the couch, and nodded to the room.

I beheld the image of serenity, depth, and self-sufficiency. He embodied freedom from suffering, ignorance, even death. A complete, self-realized human being whose mere presence implied that I, too, could be free.

After several weeks, I was at home. I had found a small community of dedicated, like-minded seekers, an intellectually sophisticated and compassionate teacher and, most of all, a simple practice that emptied my mind of trivial thoughts and filled my heart with love.

Almost without noticing it, I adopted wholesale a philosophy that ran counter to everything I had been taught: The "real" world is an illusion. The only reality is consciousness. Pure awareness, big mind, can be reached only through meditation. Enlightenment or liberation from suffering is a result of the regular experience of that.

I began to believe that the way I led my life was the source of my pain. My attachment to people and things caused my suffering. The high stimulation of my lifestyle produced the stress in my nervous system, which agitated my mind, which triggered more desires, which led to seeking more stimulation—in an endless cycle of frustration and desire.

Like a key fitting into a lock, this teaching fit into some unknown part of me, and a hole closed seamlessly around it. As this message held a growing numinosity, the rest of life held less shine. The satisfaction of desires through personal love or creative work seemed futile. Working only to save money to go to more retreats, and socializing only with people who shared my worldview and my goal of enlightenment, I burned for god.

Very quickly, the spiritual group became my new family, harmonious and aligned, unlike my family of origin. My parents, from this new perspective, seemed lost to the world of materialism; my old friends seemed lost to the illusions of politics and romance.

I read voraciously in Eastern philosophy, assimilating its ideas until they were a part of me, flesh of my flesh. I found my life purpose and, like an arrow heading for the target, went off to a long retreat, where I meditated ... and meditated ... and meditated. When my back ached and my concentration faltered, I wondered what latent, nagging, restless urge led me to shut my eyes to the beauties of the world. But then my mind quieted for a moment, dipping into a delicious silence, and the questions evaporated.

After two months of a rigorous routine, I cast aside any remaining doubts and chose to become an instructor. I could hardly believe my good fortune. Like many before, I felt chosen—and certain that I had found the Way.

Again, I attended a sitting for several months. During that time, I practiced yoga, meditated, and ate simple meals. I did not see a man; I did not get distracted by other stimuli. For all intents and purposes, I led a monastic life.

Near the end of that period, I was in an altered state of consciousness: deeply rested, yet hyper-awake inside. I did not need to sleep or dream, that is to go under into unconsciousness. Instead, the inner wakefulness simply continued, whether I was lying down or walking around.

However, something else had changed as well. When I joined this spiritual army, there were no signs of regimentation, authoritarianism, hierarchy, or even rigid adherence to dogma. Perhaps because I knew nothing of the dark side, I couldn't see it. But I believe that in its early years this organization was fairly tolerant and open-ended.

Slowly, this attitude shifted, stricter guidelines set in, and eventually an institutional hierarchy arose. There was no dramatic violation of my rights, no singular spiritual abuse from which to recover. I simply began to grow uncomfortable with what I observed in the group dynamics.

I spoke to friends about my growing discomfort. But no one wanted to hear. Growing alienated from those I loved most deeply, I began to question the teachings to which I had devoted my life. The more I questioned, the more the pain increased. And the questions kept coming:

- Why doesn't this community feel like home anymore?

- What is this gap between the group's public persona and its inner workings?

- Why doesn't anyone else admit that something is subtly wrong?

- What would my life be like without my spiritual family?

- How can I live without the hope of enlightenment or salvation?

- If I leave, can I continue to meditate, separating the practice from the organization and its beliefs?

- How do I work through the grief of having invested more than a decade of my life in this community?

Just as upon my discovery of Eastern philosophy the world had become unreal and dreamlike (maya), so now my alternative world seemed like a bad dream.

At the end of the training, I stood at a fork in the road, about to make one of those major life choices that quickly rules out other options and forms a certain destiny: to continue my cloistered life with its sole focus on raising consciousness, or to return to the quotidian world, to ordinary people and ordinary dreams. Even then, the choice seemed to mean taking only one of two directions: up to the life of spirit or down to the world of matter; up to god or down to earth.

With a heart clouded by uncertainty, I boarded the next plane home. I never took official action, but other members knew that I had stepped out of the circle. I expected my closest friends to understand; they did not. More than that, they would speak to me no more. I returned to Los Angeles an apostate, without a friend, without a job, without faith.

During the next 10 years, I suffered a deep disillusionment with the meditation community and its teachings. I slowly began to look at each philosophical assumption from every angle, turning it around and around, examining it as if my life depended not on hanging onto it, but on seeing through it. I applied the discipline of mind I had developed in meditation to questioning its premises.

I tried desperately to understand what aroused this intense longing in me, this hunger for spiritual sweets, this thirst for the nectar of the gods—this desire to dissolve. I sought answers in the twists and turns of my family dynamics and in the sweeping vision of transpersonal psychology. I studied the timeless mystical traditions in an effort to find my predecessors there—Krishna's devoted *gopis*, the dancing Bal Shem Tov, Sufi poets Rumi and Kabir, the Hindu ecstatic Mirabai, the nuns for god Catherine of Siena and Julian of Norwich.

And, although my disillusionment with my teacher and his teachings was heart-wrenching, I suffered an even deeper disillusionment with god who, I believed, set me on the path only to betray me. For a long time, I railed at my god, pointing a finger of blame at the heavens.

I had believed that a spiritual commitment would save me from shadow suffering. Like a child who believes that if she prays fervently enough, her petitions will come true, I thought that if I meditated diligently enough, fulfillment would result. And not only that: fulfillment without sacrifice.

I had held a simple image of the spiritual path—do your daily practice, purify your lifestyle, open your heart in love—which ended in certain rewards. How was it possible that my practices, my devotions, would leave me with empty arms? How was it possible that god would give me stone when I had earned bread?

I fell headlong into a well of despair, slipping into the underworld that I had struggled so hard to evade. I disappeared into a great blackness, living for a while at the bottom of a dark hole looking up.

Eventually, groping in the dark for a thread to lead me out, I found a guide, a Jungian analyst, who was familiar with the back streets of the underworld, a guide who knew that my next key could be found in the darkness, not in the light. She helped me to pierce the innocence that held me in thrall to my teacher, which eventually enabled me to withdraw the spiritual projection onto him and reclaim my own radiance. She helped me to dissect the simplistic framework that held me in blame, which eventually enabled me to think more independently and to hold a more complex, nuanced view of spiritual life. She introduced me to the many gods living in my own soul, so that my former conception of a singular, allmighty god appeared naïve and childlike. She initiated me into the sacred shadow side of life, where the hidden power of darkness shines like gold.

Today I see my awakening to this longing in my soul as my awakening to a conscious life, a second birth. I see it as the fuel that drives my ongoing quest for greater understanding and for ecstatic experience. I see this longing behind my other deepest longings. I see it behind my images; I hear it behind my words. I see this longing before me, before I was, and before I become. My goal is not the end of longing; the holy longing itself is my guide.

Perhaps you, too, feel a yearning beneath your other yearnings that gnaws at you, despite the fulfillment of so many other desires. Perhaps you also fled the traditional religion of your childhood and, like me, joined an alternative community hoping to find spiritual values and practices that would deepen your inner life. Or you may continue to be a believer but find yourself in exile from the traditional forms in which your faith is expressed. Or you may have suffered spiritual or religious abuse and disillusionment at the hands of teachers or clergy, resulting in a loss of faith, hope, and trust.

And yet … your holy longing stirs. You feel a restless desire for something more, but you lack the words and images to describe your quest.

I have found in my counseling work with hundreds of clients that this essential yearning—a secret feeling with many disguises—lies hidden at the source of each person's life story. It is the seed of a soul's desire, which spurs us to take certain actions, which in turn evoke more desire and again more action.

In Part I, you will read many stories of peoples' longing and how the object of our desire calls us to follow it, like a whispering echo. We respond, even unknowingly, perhaps by pursuing a romantic union that we imagine will fulfill our deepest needs. Or we seek a spiritual communion with a mediator for the divine, in a twinship that promises to surpass human limits. Or we serve a fellowship community, a dedicated group of believers who form a surrogate family in which we feel at home. In this way, the obscure object of our longing, like a hidden compass, determines the course of our lives, pointing us in its direction. And our life story unfolds, invisibly shaping our destiny from moment to moment.

I will uncover some of the invisible images at the center of the archetype of holy longing, the fantasies of the soul longing for the divine. Together, they help to account for our indescribable yearnings for something Other, something beyond the bounds of ordinary life. Like Jung, who suggested that the gods are in our own souls and appear to us spontaneously as archetypal images—the beloved parent, the beloved partner, the beloved home, the beloved teacher or god—I suggest that by contemplating our own sacred images of holy longing, we can uncover our own gods.

Is there a transcendent God blazing behind the image? That is a question for theologians and people of faith. I am not advocating a position here concerning the metaphysical reality of god. That is why I use the small "g" to indicate the divine image or *imago dei* as it lives within our souls and as it mobilizes uncanny power in our lives.

With the help of this book, you can begin to detect the whispering call of your own soul. You can begin to acknowledge your longing and to reflect on it. You can explore what fuels it and what derails it, what ignites it and what numbs it.

You can discover the particular ways that you override your religious yearning by misplacing it onto concrete objects—sex, food, drugs, and alcohol. When you fail to discriminate between these "idols" and your true object of desire, you are left feeling forever frustrated and dissatisfied. In addition, you silence the urgent message of your soul and hear only the voices of distraction, addiction, and compulsion. Instead, you can learn to attune to your holy longing, to hear its echoes of the past and its portents of the future.

In Part II, I will explore the painful the dark side of holy longing—the inherent pitfalls that can result when religious yearning goes awry. Countless recent headlines have highlighted the forces of destruction and annhilation that lie dormant in religious fundamentalisms and blind faith of all types—whether Christian, Jewish, Muslim, Hindu, Buddhist or new age. As a result, today we see the painful consequences of religious abuse and disillusionment on the faces of believers everywhere. I will attempt to shed light on this dark corner of religious life by exploring the roots of charismatic personalities, as well as those who are susceptible to them, and by uncovering universal patterns in spiritual abuse that can be used as wake-up calls for the purpose of prevention.

Clearly, the encounter with spiritual darkness throws believers into the fires of doubt. And these fires can either consume us or transform us. As Fyodor Doestoevsky put it, "The ideal passes through suffering like gold through fire."

The work of recovery, which I call spiritual shadow-work, cannot save us from suffering. It is not offered as a solution to a problem. Instead, I suggest that when we enter the night sea journey, as Jung called it, we are not off the path; we are on it. In fact, we may be spot on it, right where we belong—ready to face spiritual shadow in ourselves or others.

If that is the case, then our disillusionment or loss of faith is an innate part of the inner journey. And our psychological work to recover our faith and to reclaim parts of ourselves that were sacrificed during periods of spiritual naivete is part of the larger spiritual task. In the same way that our cultural innocence was betrayed by the events of September 11, 2001, and our religious innocence was betrayed by the epidemic allegations of abuse by Catholic clergy, each of us undergoes the betrayal of our own naivete when we face the spiritual shadow.

Next, I explore those parts of ourselves that we typically sacrifice in order to participate in a religious community or to obey spiritual doctrine. I suggest that by doing spiritual shadow-work we can reclaim those lost parts and, as the mystics of all traditions teach, becoming more whole, develop through the stages of religious innocence toward a more mature spirituality.

By doing so, we can build bridges between our emotional and our spiritual lives, which are all too often perceived as separate means for separate ends. Today the inner journey needs to include psychological growth, that is, ego development and shadow awareness, so that our spiritual practices can be augmented with the safeguards of psychology.

But psychological growth and spiritual awakening are not the same animal; spiritual shadow-work does not lead inexorably to enlightenment. In the final section of this book, we move through the shadow to the light—through the deafening betrayal and heartbreaking disillusionment, back to the continuing longing of our souls, and ultimately onward to the end point of evolution itself—union with the source.

In the new epilogue to this edition, I share a few of my discoveries since finding and befriending a number of awake people. And I preview a bit about the myths of enlightenment that many seekers hold and that will be the topic of my next book.

To sum up, this book explores the deeply felt desire for union with the divine in whatever faith or language it appears in you. This hidden yearning lies at the root of religious belief and faith. It is the heart of religion, not the mind. It is a *feeling* for the eternal, a taste of the infinite that sweetly lingers or emotionally seizes us with rapture or despair.

Religion, wrote William James, is the feelings, acts, and experiences of individuals as they stand in relation to whatever they consider the divine. Theologies grow out of these felt experiences, he added. And I suggest that it is the strength of these feelings of yearning and desire, longing and hope that determines the degree of our religiosity and the depth of our soul's desire.

This book will not examine the content of theological or philosophical beliefs. Instead, it examines the inner worlds of those who feel holy longing, the experience of the holy, which promises participation in the greater mystery. Therefore, as the inside story of religious longing, it cuts across denominations and links them to a more universal experience.

William James also wrote that as an individual grows in self-awareness, she may begin to be influenced by another dimension through a longing or desire for it: "There is an unseen order and our supreme good lies in harmoniously adjusting ourselves [to it]. This belief and this adjustment are the religious attitude in the soul."

This inherent need of the soul—to turn to face the holy and to be changed by an experience of it—is purposeful and meaningful, according to Carl Jung. It is an inborn striving to open our limited personal selves to the archetypal and transpersonal realms. Just as Freud posited a will to pleasure, Adler wrote of a will to power, Frankel advocated a will to meaning, and Maslow postulated a will to self-actualization, I suggest that there also lies within us a will to transcend, a longing for the eternal.

Although psychology is my lens, this book does not reduce spirituality to psychology or reduce the ineffable to words. Instead, I intend to use psychology to explore spirituality, rather than to explain it. I believe that our early personal histories and unmet emotional needs influence our adult spiritual quests and religious desires. They are a necessary part of our exploration, but not a sufficient explanation.

The same is true for biology. In the early part of the last century, before the advent of neuroscience, William James pointed out that "medical materialism" attributes St. Paul's conversion to an occipital lesion due to epilepsy, St. Teresa's ecstatic visions to hysteria, and St. Francis of Assisi's asceticism to a bad gene. Today we know that there are neurobiological correlates to our emotional experiences, such as depression and anxiety. And there are brain correlates to heightened spiritual experiences as well.

In *Why God Won't Go Away,* neuroscientist Andrew Newberg described using brain-scan technology to map the inner worlds of Tibetan Buddhists in meditation and Franciscan nuns in prayer. Whether the subjects called their experiences loss of self or unity with god, respectively, they felt a sense of transcendence when activity in the frontal lobes increased and activity in the parietal lobes (which define our feeling of orientation to a physical self) decreased. That is, when this latter area is deprived of information for drawing a line between self and other, we feel a sense of boundless awareness.

This machinery of transcendence can be set in motion by ritual behaviors such as chanting, singing, and drumming, as well as prayer and meditation. That's why, Newburg concluded, god won't go away even in our age of reason.

Hard-core rationalists may use this data to support the thesis that god is merely a perception generated by the human brain. Hard-core religionists might argue that these findings offer evidence that the brain is wired to experience the a priori reality of god. But I suggest that neuroscience has not explained away the mystery after all. Biological correlations are not the same as causes. The soul's longing is embodied, perhaps even wired into the brain. But that doesn't mean it's caused by fleeting chemical events in the bodymind, even though it is reflected in those events. Thus the revelations of high-tech brain images can deepen, rather than dispel the mystery of god in the human brain.

At the same time, this book does not romanticize spiritual experience by singing its praises and cleansing it of all dangers and darkness. Instead, it aims to acknowledge the pervasiveness and worthiness of our holy longing and to place it in the broader and deeper context of human evolution: you will see that your soul's desire is not separate from the vastness of life, but that it participates as an innate and vital part of it.

Archetypal psychologist James Hillman posed a guiding question for this book: What does the soul want? He suggested that the soul wants something that is not what we think it wants. So, we seek the wrong thing—money, power, sex, food, alcohol, drugs—and turn up empty-handed. We are left, again and again, with the ineffable, the mystery. And our yearning burns in us.

Words—such as *holy longing*—evoke feelings and images that activate meaning for us. When I first saw those two words in the title of Goethe's poem, I felt startled. He had found language to signify what I had always felt: my longing *was* holy; my longing was *for* the holy. The words lived in me for many years before this book was born.

In this way, words act as potent symbols that bridge the known to the unknown. As Russell Lockhart put it, words are eggs. They crack open, giving birth to new forms of life.

For this reason, an examination of the roots of words, their invisible histories and multiple meanings, can be helpful in uncovering what the soul wants. Donna Marie Flanagan, in an unpublished thesis for the Chicago Jung Institute, examined the root meanings of *longing*, "to feel a strong desire or craving, especially for something not likely to be attained." She pointed out that even this basic definition conveys an image of distance in time or space. It also implies that the one who is longing is discontent.

Yearning, a cousin of longing, means to long persistently, wistfully, or sadly. It's related to a Latin word meaning to cause to wish. It's also related to a Greek word that means grateful and is tied to the word eucharist, the holy sacrament. Therefore, Flanagan said, yearning is related to a wish being caused by an Other and also to being gratified by a symbol of the divine.

To crave has its roots in to demand, which is linked to craft. A visceral craving that counters the ego's rationality requires our craftiness to satisfy it. Flanagan pointed out that craving brings to mind hunger and thirst, which are common images of longing.

When we glean these root meanings of *longing*, we can contemplate again the question: what does the soul want? And we can understand more deeply the hidden power of religious yearning. It does not involve finding the object of our desire and satisfying our hunger, like being satiated after a rich meal. Rather, it means holding the tension of our longing, returning it again and again to our own souls, so that ultimately it may reveal its secrets and lead us to the next level of consciousness. It means tracking spiritual desire like a faint footprint, not to trap an object but to catch its scent and follow it deeper into the landscape of the soul.

Although at times it may be frustrating and even painful to hold the tension of your yearning rather than to submerge it, when you align with it you align with the force of evolution itself.

And my wish for every reader is that your holy longing guide you home.

PART I

Before the Fall:
A Guide for Faithful
Believers

One thing have I desired of the Lord, that will I seek after: that I may dwell in the house of the Lord all the day of my life, to behold the beauty of the Lord, and to inquire in his temple.

—Psalm 27

Those who constantly cherish only intense longing to encounter the essential face of their lord will attain complete realization.

—Koran 92:20-21

I long for a single glance from your eyes of pure love. To you alone I consecrate my entire existence without ceasing.

—A Hindu sacred hymn

A Hasidic rabbi noticed that an old man didn't follow the meaning of his discourse. He summoned the man and told him to listen to a melody instead. The rabbi hummed a song without words, a poignant melody of trust in god and of clinging to him. The old man proclaimed, "Now I understand what you wish to teach. I feel an intense longing to be united with the Lord."

—A Hasidic tale

1

The Holy Longing

In every mystical tradition, saints and lovers speak eloquently of the soul's search for the beloved, its yearning for the gods, its longing for communion. The bride in the Hebrews' Song of Solomon sings her erotic yearning for her bridegroom, desiring to kiss him because his love is better than wine. The bride proclaims fervent union at last: "My beloved is mine, and I am his." Her triumphant proclamation recalls the cries of Christian mystics such as Julian of Norwich: "We are in God and God, whom we do not see, is in us."

The Greek *maenads*, or mad women, dressed in fawns skins and ivy crowns, carried lit torches and danced wildly around Dionysus, desiring nothing but union with him. The Egyptian Queen, Isis, lamented and longed for her murdered husband, Osiris. After finding his body parts and rejoining them, she united with him. Osiris was resurrected a god, king of the dead. In the Hindu tradition of devotion, milkmaids, known as *gopis,* long for union with Krishna, the dark blue god. Krishna's sixteenth-century devotee, Mirabai, wanted to be turned into a heap of incense, burned into ash, and smeared on his chest.

I wonder why the metaphor of burning recurs again and again in the words of mystics, saints, and devotional poets to attempt to describe the ardor of human-divine love. St. John of the Cross said he was fired by love's urgent longings for Christ, the divine beloved. Jewish mystics declare that burning ecstasy unlocks the meaning of life. If we fulfill the commandments but don't feel the burning, they say, we won't feel it in paradise. Thirteenth-century Sufi poet Jelaluddin Rumi declared that a burning of the heart is more precious than everything else because it calls god secretly in the dark.

More recently, eminent psychologist Carl Jung proclaimed: "A man who is not on fire is nothing; he is ridiculous, he is two-dimensional. He must be on fire even if he does make a fool of himself. A flame must burn somewhere, otherwise no light shines, there is no warmth, there is nothing."

The master poet Goethe spoke of it in "The Holy Longing" when he said,

Tell a wise person, or else keep silent,
because the massman will mock it right away.
I praise what is truly alive,
what longs to be burned to death.

In the calm waters of the love-nights,
where you were begotten, where you have begotten,
a strange feeling comes over you
when you see the silent candle burning.
Now you are no longer caught
in the obsession with darkness,
and a desire for higher love-making
sweeps you upward.

Distance does not make you falter,
now, arriving in magic, flying,
and, finally, insane for the light,
you are the butterfly and you are gone.

And so long as you haven't experienced this:
to die and so to grow,
you are only a troubled guest
on the dark earth. (Trans. by Robert Bly)

I suggest that it is because of this holy longing for something Other, this timeless yearning for union with something beyond ourselves, that human beings sit still, cross-legged, eyes closed, as the splendors of spring pass us by. It is because of this longing that we strive to lose ourselves in one another in ecstatic embrace, like Shiva and Shakti weaving creation. It is because of this longing that we build Sistine Chapels, sculpt the David, and compose the Messiah. It is even because of it that we search intensively for the smallest bit of matter, the "god particle," which might be the ultimate building block of life.

It is also because of this holy longing that Islamic fundamentalists fighting a *jihad,* or holy war, eagerly sacrifice their lives to go to paradise. It is because of this longing that cult fanatics, such as those at Jamestown, commit group suicide to attain the other world. It is because of this longing that monks and nuns wall off the difficult demands of bodily life and bury their emotional wisdom like hidden treasure. It is because of this longing that faithful churchgoers and aspiring meditators refuse to see what appears before them as spiritual abuse, perpetrated in the name of god.

In my earlier book *Romancing the Shadow* (with Steve Wolf), I explored several forms of human longing: the longing for family soul, the yearning for the ideal partner, the desire for the sacred friend, the hope for meaningful work, and the search for meaning at midlife. In *The Holy Longing*, I explore an even more primary hunger: the drive toward self-transcendence that fuels evolution itself in the physical, mental, and spiritual worlds.

In the physical realm, for example, those physicists who developed thermodynamics observed that physical systems tend to deteriorate, moving from order to disorder, like a car becoming a heap of rust. But a more recent theory suggests that a self-organizing capacity, which was previously invisible, is inherent in physical systems. Nobel prize winner Ilya Prigogine demonstrated that open systems are characterized by self-organization, self-renewal, and self-transcendence. Although simple physical systems appear to fall apart, some actually fall together, transcending their previous level of development and reorganizing at a higher level.

The sciences of complexity suggest that the end point of a physical system pulls its development in that direction: an acorn inevitably becomes an oak, a zygote grows into a human being. When a system becomes unstable and chaotic, an internal force (known as an attractor) reconfigures it for a new and higher level of stability. The system unfolds according to its end point, driven toward greater levels of integration by the physical analogue of the holy longing.

In the mental realm, the holy longing is at work in individual development as the soul longs for manifestation. It attaches to form and conception takes place, beginning the downward journey from unconscious unity to ego consciousness, the journey toward a separate self.

Pre-personal stages of individual development find their fulfillment in the personal stage of a fully consolidated ego. For most psychologists, this is the goal or end point of human growth, exemplified in the myth of the hero who follows his path alone, combats his adversaries, and ultimately wins a boon.

But for mystics of all traditions and for transpersonal psychologists and philosophers, who intuit the larger story of the holy longing, this moment is another stage in the cycle of consciousness: the beginning of what the Sufis call "the great return." The holy longing is transformed from a yearning for separation and individuality to a yearning for ego transcendence and union.

In the spiritual realm, this will to transcend is built into the human soul as spiritual aspiration. This yearning can be felt as a restless hunger to unite with a holy Other, something greater than ourselves. It drives the *telos* or direction of the journey from ego consciousness to Self realization, from personal to transpersonal life, just as the silkworm emerges a butterfly, to use St. Teresa's metaphor.

Christian mystic Meister Eckhart put it this way: "Now the seed of god is in us. The seed of a pear tree grows into a pear tree. The seed of god grows into god." Or as Rabbi Heschel put it, "There is the grain of the prophet in the recesses of every human life." Buddhists teach this too: they believe that a seed of Buddhahood lies at the core of every sentient being, and its realization is the end point of our evolution.

The glories of the "downward" arc of involution—from unconscious transcendence to immanence in incarnation—have been extolled by scientists and psychologists for hundreds of years. The glories of the "upward" arc of evolution—from immanence to conscious transcendence in enlightenment—have been extolled by poets, spiritual teachers and mystics for thousands of years.

But warring camps have emerged. In *Sex, Ecology, Spirituality*, Ken Wilber calls those who favor "up" puritannical ascenders, who tend to devalue nature, the body, and the senses. And he calls those who favor "down" shadow-hugging descenders, who futilely seek the timeless in the world of time.

Rarely does a philosopher present the full cycle. Hasidic rabbi Schneur Zalman described the big picture when he wrote in the mystical *Tanya*: "The process leading from god to man is one of materializing the spiritual; that leading from man to god one of spiritualizing the material."

Wilber pointed out that Plato also saw the full cycle: he traced the outflowing of the One through god into the world of Forms and into human minds, then bodies, then matter. He also traced the return journey of the soul from its infatuation with the material realm through the mental realm of Forms to a spiritual immersion in the One.

However, his descending vision became associated with the dark shadows of the cave. As a result, the ascending vision became the goal of Western civilization: up and away from the flesh toward spirit; up and away from the world toward heaven. Aristotle, Augustine, Hegel, Schopenhauer, de Chardin, Novalis, Coleridge, and others perpetuated that bias, with devastating long-range consequences: the devaluation of nature, the body, and the feminine.

The ascending and descending paths also appear in microcosm in us in our *kundalini*, a subtle energy that is imagined in Tantric yoga and Oriental medicine as a serpent coiled at the base of the spine, which ascends to the top of the head with meditation practice. As it rises, the *kundalini* opens the seven *charkas,* which are energy vortices that attract life force from its source. At each level, the *chakra* acts as an interface between individual awareness and the energy frequencies of that level. As *kundalini* energy is activated and *chakras* open, the individual incorporates ever-higher frequencies into the self, as it identifies with each level and is transformed by it.

Yoga masters have mapped the progress of energy up from primitive stages in the lower *chakras* to reunion with its divine source in the highest or crown *chakra.* In ancient China, Taoist masters taught "circulation of the light," in which sexual energy is generated in the lower spine, sent up to the top of the head to become spiritualized, and directed back down the spine to complete a circle and begin again.

The holy longing fuels the ascent of *kundalini*—the upward arc—as the individual longs for higher levels of unity. At the same time, the magnetic pull of the higher *chakras* draws up the evolving self.

Conversely, the holy longing fuels the descent—the downward arc—as the individual yearns for embodiment, sexual union, and immanence. The magnetic pull of the lower *charkas* draws down the evolving self.

I suggest that by making conscious the descent, development, and ascent of the soul, we can participate more consciously in evolution. Through allying with our holy longing, rather than resisting it, we can learn to hear the call of the soul. Through fidelity to our yearning, rather than betrayal, we can fuel evolution in our own lives and in the life of our species. This is the greatest promise of uncovering and attending to our religious yearning: our will to transcend aligns us with the collective drive toward self-transcendence.

Awakening to holy longing

A famous Jewish mystic, Rabbi Abraham Kook, pointed out that the person who tries to sustain himself only from the surface of life will suffer terrible impoverishment. "Then he will feel, welling up within himself, a burning thirst for that inner substance and vision that transcends the obvious surfaces. From such inner resources he will seek the waters of joy that can quicken the dry outer skeleton of life."

This innate burning thirst can be felt in many ways. For some, the holy longing can be detected as a nagging awareness of a lack or a fleeting sense of something more. At 50, one woman sat across from me with a challenging glare: "I feel a constant, gnawing ache inside. Time is passing. I *know* this is not all there is."

Her statement implied unspoken questions begging for answers. I recalled Jung declaring that every patient he saw over the age of 35 was suffering from a religious problem. My client's pressing desire for something more pointed to her unconscious need for meaning and value, a need that was essentially religious because it revolved around her relation to larger forces, higher powers, or what we may call the gods.

Early childhood experiences of abuse, grief, and loss lead many people to seek relief from suffering, but more as well: caught in feelings of anger and bitterness, they seek compassion and forgiveness. Trapped in feelings of isolation, they seek communion. Entering therapy to minister to past wounds, they begin to ask spiritual questions of meaning and depth. The pain that had seemed so purposeless and arbitrary is the very thing that sets them on the path.

Other people hear what mystics refer to as the still, quiet voice, or what the Sufis refer to as the call of the beloved. After that, they intuit that this world of the senses is not all there is. They wander restlessly from place to place, relationship to relationship, church to church, guru to guru. Their relentless hunger drives them here and there, but the smorgasbord of tastes never satisfies.

Many people experience their longing as a yearning for romantic love. Their hunger for the ideal loved one compels them to place relationship on the altar, above all other things. And, believing in the sacred power of love to heal them, even to save them, they anoint the lover with special gifts and unknowingly ask him or her to stand in for the divine.

Some women long for a divine child to redeem them. I have met women who, since their own youth, have yearned for the birth of a special child whose unconditional love will reward them. Or, disillusioned with a romantic beloved, a parent may unconsciously channel holy longing toward an innocent child, who becomes the family savior.

Others set their longing in a spiritual framework and feel it as a yearning for the light, which compels them to purify themselves of darkness. They may attempt to achieve this through strict diets and fasting or yoga and meditation. They may seek a teacher who is ahead of them on the path and who can relieve them of sins through practice or good deeds. They may imagine their objective as a desired shift in consciousness, which offers an end to isolation through a direct experience of unity with all of life.

As good Buddhists, they may give up their back support and sit upright for extra hours of meditation practice. As good Christians, they may redouble their efforts to take up the cross and follow Christ. As good Jews, they may strive harder to fulfill the commandments with the proper intention. As good Muslims, they may recommit to following the *Shari'a*, or sacred law. In each case, believers channel their fervor into form, turning it into an effort toward greater perfection, a striving toward a remote goal. And the form of their striving is determined by the form of the holy Other, the object of their desire.

For some, the goal is an ideal home, either a community of like-minded seekers or a paradise in the other world. Many mythic heroes—Odysseus, Gilgamesh, Dionysus, Heracles—are wanderers who follow a restless urge that never finds its object. James Hillman referred to this urge as *pothos*, the longing toward the unattainable, ungraspable something that drives our seeking for home.

This motif of paradise recurs in every generation: in an earlier time, human beings lived in unity with the creator and in harmony with nature. The Hindu's Vedic age of enlightened seers, the Hebrew garden of Eden, the Greek golden age, the Viking warriors' Valhalla, the Australian aboriginal dreamtime, the Chinese Taoist age of perfect virtue, the Muslim paradise in which the Prophet awaits his martyrs. All are local variations on the universal theme of a long, lost time and place of perfection.

Some traditions encourage a longing for this other world. It can be felt in the poignant yearning of black Gospel music for Jesus and his salvation. It can be seen in schools of Jewish mysticism that teach that a believer who does not savor the world to come, but whose soul still yearns and thirsts for god, will not quench his thirst with the water of the Torah that is in front of him. Rather, he is like a man who stands in a river and cries for water to drink.

Even today this image of paradise—home and happiness—beckons us with archetypal power. But it may remain just outside the boundaries of our awareness. Like a forgotten hypnotic suggestion, it compels us to leave home to find home, and yet it remains hidden from sight. Perhaps, as some literal thinkers believe, its source is a memory of history, an actual time and place. Or perhaps, more symbolically, paradise harks back to an earlier psychological state.

Freud spoke of it as a return to the womb. In his early work, Jung thought it stemmed from a desire for the forbidden parent, which can never attain its goal. Therefore, we long eternally for the unattainable. Later, he viewed it as the ego yearning for the Self, the archetype of wholeness. Transpersonal psychologists believe it refers to a future level of consciousness that we have not yet achieved as a species.

For a select few, an object of longing appears at once, as in Paul's revelation of blinding light on the road to Damascus, or Dante's sighting of the young Beatrice, or Ram Dass's instantaneous recognition of his Indian master, or St. Catherine's first vision of Jesus. That vision takes over the emotional life of the person like a possession. For example, Paul, formerly a Jew who fought against the teachings of Jesus, became the main advocate for a life in Christ.

When this happens, all earlier commitments are relativized. Dante contemplated the image of Beatrice as his anima, or soul image, for years to come. And she fired the poet's imagination.

And all former values lose their foundation. Richard Alpert, a professor at Harvard, became Ram Dass and spent his life teaching the value of Indian mystical practices. For Paul, Dante, Ram Dass, and St. Catherine, meaning gathered around the beloved object like iron filings around a magnet.

For some, the holy longing is felt with the sweetness of hope and the ideal of communion with others. "I long for a community of souls," a friend said, "where I'm like one lit firefly among thousands in the dark skies."

For others, it is suffered with the bitterness of isolation and disillusionment. An encounter with our lower nature, our sins or shadows, may evoke a deep desire for repentance and healing. When we see our own cruelty or face our unconscious limitations for the first time, we may yearn for the light of consciousness and the forgiveness of higher forces.

As we awaken to our longing for transcendence, our love of family may seem to bind us to attachments and responsibilities, which keep us tethered to this world. Work may feel purposeless and seem to separate us from our higher aims. Our human limits and longings for material comfort and love seem to conflict with our religious yearnings. And the object of our longing appears forever elusive, trapping us in promises for the future and robbing us of the vitality of the present moment.

"It's always out there, in front of me, just out of reach," a client said. "I feel no gratitude for what is, only hope for what should be and fear that it will never come."

Finally, many individuals turn a deaf ear to the whispers of the soul. Myths tell us of heroes who do not heed the call. Today, too, despite their spiritual thirst, some people retrench in established patterns, too fearful to risk changing a life of comfort. Or they find substitute gratification in alcohol, drugs, or sex, which appear to quench their thirst for a moment. But their holy longing is simply held captive in a substance. On the other hand, stories of the mystics and saints in every tradition give us a glimpse into the lives of those who follow their longing to its source.

God longs for us as we long for god

The inner urge that sets us seeking is itself the thing we are looking for.

—Karlfried Graf Durckheim

Like the individual soul longing for manifestation and completion on the downward arc, creation myths tell us that the unmanifest god desired manifestation—and spirit descended into matter. Some religions view "down" as a fall from grace, an irreparable loss of original unity. But if we keep in mind the complete cycle of consciousness, as the mystical traditions tend to do, we see that it is only one half of the story: descent into matter is occurring simultaneously and continuously with ascent to spirit. Unconscious unity is leading to conscious unity everywhere and always.

In Hinduism, Brahma, the creator, manifested life to dispel the enveloping darkness. He created the waters and deposited a seed that became a golden egg, which was divided into male and female. For Hindu mystics, the purpose of life is to realize consciously the unity that was present in the beginning unconsciously.

Hindu myths of gods and goddesses retell this universal narrative of the human soul, often depicted as feminine, longing for the divine beloved, portrayed as masculine. For example, the milkmaid Radha adores her consort Krishna, an incarnation of god. He performs super-human feats to destroy the powers of evil and is renowned for his skill as a flute player. When he plays, spreading the melodies of love through the cow pastures, peacocks strut, cows adore him, clouds let the rain fall. And Radha and the other devotees dance about him, burning for his love.

From a human level of interpretation, Radha, a woman married to another man, directs her fervor to an unattainable object of desire, in apparent disregard for social convention. As in the courtly love tradition of English troubadours, it is the lovers' separateness that fuels their desire for union.

From another level of interpretation, Radha is the ultimate female devotee, or *bhakta*, who seeks complete identification with her image of god. At this level, there is no question of morality, but of a worshipper's desire for union with her beloved or, more symbolically, a soul's desire for union with god.

Finally, from the point of view of unity, Radha and Krishna never were separate. Pure consciousness or spirit divided itself into two—Krishna and Radha or the masculine and feminine face of god—only in our limited perception or level of consciousness. In the final stages, duality is an illusion.

In Jewish mysticism, the light of the absolute source, or *ein sof,* descended, degree by degree, into the world through many "garments," which screened its light, until the material world emerged as darkness embodied. The purpose of this downward gradation of light into creation is transformative: one day, with the coming of the Messiah, the light of the *ein sof* will shine in the place of greatest darkness.

But this fulfillment depends upon human action. When believers follow the commandments with the proper intention, or *kavanah,* they bring down the light from above into matter, which was previously dark. The *Tanya* tells them that their hearts should truly desire this higher union—the joining of the soul with the light of god—and that they should habituate themselves to this intention, which puts them into harmony with god's will.

Jewish prayer is in part a crying out of holy longing to god, a calling for the divine presence to come nearer. As Psalm 141 says, "Lord, I cry unto thee: make haste unto me; give ear to my voice when I cry unto thee. Let my prayer be set forth before thee as incense and the lifting up of my hands as the evening sacrifice."

In addition, when believers focus on learning the Torah they intend to bind their thought to god's thought, their speech to god's speech. And they call to the holy one to come closer, just as a person calls a companion or a child calls a father to join her and end their separation. As Psalm 145 puts it, "The Lord is nigh to all that call unto him."

As the Kabbalah put it, in the beginning, there was only god. With an in-breath, it withdrew into itself and, contracting, left a space where there was no god. With an out-breath, God reentered that space. During this process, the light of god scattered: some holy sparks returned to their source; others fell into the mineral, vegetable, animal, and human realms, destroying the original divine harmony. Those sparks that fell forever yearn to return.

It is the human task to repair divine unity by lifting the sparks through our deeds, which are spelled out in the commandments. This work of repair, or *tikkun,* is the hidden purpose of Jewish life, and it may carry us far into the darkness of descent. Some Hasids suggest that gathering those sparks that have fallen farthest from god is the greatest *tikkun.* However, this task also presents the greatest danger: the risk of getting lost in the darkness.

This Jewish story of individual mission parallels the collective story of Jewish life: as god withdrew initially, some Jews suffer the absence of god now. This condition of exile in the soul is like the exile of god from the world. For believers, this exile requires the mission of gathering sparks. The longing for god is proof of the possibility of reunion.

In the last century, Rabbi Nachman of Bratslav, who suffered a perpetual, restless yearning, told his followers that a person can shout very loudly to god in the silence of her own small inner voice. And no one will hear her because no sound is emitted. Therefore, she can stand among many people and cry out loudly, longing for god. Even today, when we sit in a synagogue during services and listen to the ancient melodies, we can hear the soul's bittersweet yearning to end separation, to climb to the higher realms, and to return home to the holy land.

Reb Nachman believed that this spiritual restlessness was a sign that a renewed effort was now required to reach another level of consciousness. For him, to sin meant to remain on the same level for too long. He would repent and beg god's forgiveness for not attaining a higher rung on the ladder. And, for him, this process meant that he was moving with the will of the universe, or the natural course of progress in the human soul. As Reb Nachman put it, "By feeling the pain and longing, yearning to be again face to face with his Holy Presence, one creates a bond that raises him high."

In Christianity, Paul spoke (in Philippians 3) about *epektasis,* reaching forth to the things that are before us and forgetting the things that are behind. We might interpret Paul's description of dying each day (in 1 Corinthians) as transcending the level of the past and being reborn to a new consciousness.

Early Christian saint Gregory of Nyssa wrote commentaries about *epektasis,* which he translated as straining toward god. For Gregory, this human effort, which stems from free will, takes place within the context of the soul's movement of perpetual ascent toward god, who is immovable. The soul is drawn by desire for god like a lover is drawn to the scent of the beloved, as described in the Song of Songs. Or, as Philippians 3 put it, he who always stretches forward will never cease his ascent, ever guided to comprehend transcendent reality.

Later, Benedict's Rule prescribed behavior that led to a monk's sharing in the sufferings of Christ so that he deserved to share in his kingdom. But these behaviors are empty without straining forward with hope in Christ, by whose spirit we participate through grace in the nature of god. And as his divine image is restored in us, we are ever more capable of giving and receiving love.

Contemporary Christian teacher Gordon Dalby takes a more psychological approach to god the Father. He told me that most Christians don't acknowledge their holy longing because, as children, they called out for their father and he failed them. He may even have scolded them—"Stop crying or I'll give you something to cry about"—when they yearned for him.

"Our fathers didn't come when we called, so we learned not to trust them. Some of us awaited their arrival with fear and dread. As a result, it's not safe to long for god the Father today. It's not safe to be like a little child, dependent on god. But that's exactly what we need for healing. Rather than choosing out of pride to be our own masters, we need to become a child who is dependent on Him, to take his saving hand, and to surrender to his plan. He will forgive us and restore us to life."

On the other hand, chaplain Jeff Utter told me that for some people the disappointment in our fathers only increases our longing for god. The reason we feel unsafe in turning to god, he said, is our fear of what god will ask of us.

This unconscious intent—to meet an absent father/god via religion—plays out in other traditions as well. The Biblical story of God's abandonment of Ishmael has led some scholars to view Islam as a tradition of orphans in search of a lost father, Allah.

In Islam, Allah is the hidden treasure who longs to be known. A longing arises spontaneously within the hiddenness of Allah's transcendence and without disturbing its perfect unity. This divine longing is the first light to emerge from the source of light. It shines prior to time and prior to eternity. It gazes everywhere, perceiving only divine unity illuminated by its own light. It calls out, "*il ilaha illallah*: There is nothing other than Allah."

The individual Sufi's journey is symmetrical: When divine yearning emerges, one begins the great return, the path of the soul from union with god through the Sufi stations (or levels of consciousness) to reunion with god, in which one consciously realizes that there is nothing other than Allah.

We can recognize these ideas in the lived realities of seekers and saints, in their narrative stories of poignant yearning for the divine beloved. Whether Christian, Jew, Hindu, Buddhist, or Sufi; whether theistic or non-theistic, they long for union with something transcendent, something beyond themselves.

The Inner Marriage: A story of holy longing in the Sufi poet Rumi

In the year 1207, in what is now Afghanistan, a boy was born to a family of Sufis, those Muslim mystics who call themselves lovers of god. As an infant in his mother's arms, Jelaloddin heard stories of the Prophet and his saints. As a toddler at his father's side, he learned to keep the names of god between his teeth, to repeat "Allah" with every breath.

One morning following the dawn prayer, seven-year-old Jelaloddin felt restless. The open sky beckoned him. He stretched out on a grassy knoll, arms flung wide, the green carpet prickly beneath his muslin pants, the sun bathing him in warmth. A circle of cypress swayed around him. He gazed up at the feathery wisps of white and watched them float freely, thinning to invisibility, and dissolving into the blue canopy. He imagined that he too could rise, float, and hover above the hills.

Just then, his body seemed to float up and the mud brick houses below receded into miniatures. He rose higher, became cloud, then air, then nothing—yet everything at once, a wind through all things, a spirit.

An ant bit his ankle and the sting jolted him back to himself. His head felt heavy on the ground, his bare neck itchy, his throat scratchy with thirst. He had ascended to the celestial world! He had known god's grace.

The mystical flight stirred a spiritual yearning in Jelaloddin, which Sufis call *himma*. It slowly detached him from the passions of other men, from the wanting animal that lives in the body and keeps men tied to earth. It helped him to still his desires from an early age—except for the desire to lift off and dissolve. And his spiritual wanting became an ardent desire for god, a passion for Him alone.

The community of Sufis left their home and wandered for many years, finally settling in the town of Konya in south-central Turkey. When Jelal was 24, his father, who was also his teacher and guide, left this world for the next. He inherited his father's pulpit, his disciples, his position of great influence. Secretly, he knew that although he was intellectually prepared, spiritually he was a novice. He felt a gnawing discontent, a yearning for something more. His wife did not fill this hole. His sons didn't fill it. His knowledge didn't fill it. Even his practices of ablutions, prayer, and fasting were not enough.

For 13 years Jelaloddin fulfilled his duty. He cared for his followers' spiritual lives by leading prayers, interpreting religious law, resolving conflicts, and mediating for them with local sultans. When his father died, he stood on the pulpit before the community and gave a sermon for the first time. From that day on, he was known as Rumi, after the land of Rum, whose residents he guided.

But one afternoon, as he rode his donkey through the streets, surrounded by his loyal followers in tattered blue robes, their questions darting about him like arrows, their turbans bobbing, he felt particularly restless. No one among them knew of his secret longing; no one among them could still it.

Suddenly, a wild desert dervish appeared out of nowhere and grabbed the reins of the donkey. The dervish, his head and eyebrows shaven clean, was dressed in rags covered with road dust. He wore a black cloak and a pointed felt hat and carried a massive wooden staff. His gray hawk eyes probed Rumi's.

The dervish stepped closer and asked an impertinent question. When Rumi responded, the stranger cried, "Praise God!"

Rumi slipped from the prickly back of the donkey and fell with a thud to the ground. He gazed up at feathery wisps of white floating freely, thinning and dissolving into the blue canopy. Just then, his body seemed to float up and hover above the hills, the men and shops below receding into miniatures. He rose higher, becoming cloud, then pure air, then nothing—yet everything at once, a wind through all things, a spirit.

The dervish came forward, lifted his wooden staff into the air, and touched Rumi between the eyebrows. Rumi felt his body jolt against the hard ground. A blazing heat rose up his spine and burst into a white light in his forehead.

A moment later, his neck itched against the gritty dirt. He lifted his head to see the dervish towering above him. Rumi recognized the man, though he had never seen him before. He rose and, without bothering to look around, took the stranger's hand and marched off with him.

From that day, Rumi stepped off the path of knowledge and onto the path of love. From that day, he knew that his rank, his knowledge, his family were all veils that separated him from god. The dervish would wear for him the face of god, and he would become a servant of love.

In the presence of the dervish, sitting knee to knee, it was easy for Rumi to love. No wanting, no striving, no wishing for this love to be different—but as it was, here, now. Rumi began to wonder if his devotion to the dervish was merely a human attachment. Was he a secret idolater? Or was he seeing the face of Allah in the dervish?

When the dervish disappeared without a trace, Rumi's life became a hymn of homesickness. If his beloved was in Damascus, then Damascus was home. If he was in Samarkand, then it was the only sanctuary. Rumi longed to see him with every fiber of his life. He yearned for the sharp clarity of that voice, the tapping sound of that staff, the scent of musk coming around the corner. And as he longed for the dervish, he longed for god. As he burned for him, he burned for Him. Everything else was gone—but this *himma*, this yearning for Him.

Distraught and alone in a dark room, his green robe and turban tossed aside, Rumi lit a small taper, which cast an arc of light on the ceiling. Suddenly, unbidden images flooded him like a storm whipping through his house. They poured down in a ceaseless rain. He swooned at their hidden meanings. He folded his legs beneath him on a cushion and contemplated the inner images as they arose, entering each one's mood and landscape.

When he opened his mouth, verses flamed out. Rumi, the scholar, was long gone. The wise man, who once thought poetry was a waste of time, was taken over by these images, the pawn of a greater force.

Eventually, Rumi's loyal son found the dervish and brought him back to Konya. Again, Rumi sat face to face with his beloved, his gaze lost in those bottomless pools. Again, he rose to the sound of the dervish's viol and turned and turned on his left foot, his arms in the air like wings.

And again the dervish disappeared. The color drained from Rumi's face. He refused food and became as thin as the dervish's staff. He refused work and wandered aimlessly through town. He ran to the city gates and accosted every visitor, without the customary greeting of peace, demanding the whereabouts of his beloved. A current of grief wrapped itself around his body.

At home he paced the room that had belonged to the dervish. Everything remained in its place: the rugs piled neatly, a few clothes in bundles. It was all there—except him. All at once, Rumi could hear *his* footsteps growing louder as they neared. He could hear the tapping of *his* staff as it touched the floor—tap, pause, tap, pause. He rose and turned toward the curtain, arms open, expecting to see him standing there. But nothing. No one. Silence.

Forty days later, he ordered mourning robes and ripped open his shirt at the chest. He stepped into the garden, placed his right hand around a post, and began to turn round and round, whispering a name of god. He leaned into the movement. The post beneath his hand disappeared. He gave himself up to the whirling and verses, swift and startling, poured out of him.

As Rumi whirled and vanished, he became still inside. His spiritual exile was coming to an end. In the first separation from his beloved, a poet was born. That longing, that burning for the beloved gripped him and drove the poems out of him. But desire remained—desire for the beloved.

Now, he died even to that desire. His beloved was in him; he was in his beloved. His gaze turned inward toward the brilliance of a million suns. (See *A Moth to the Flame* for the fully fleshed out version of Rumi's life story.)

I suggest, then, that there is an archetypal basis for the spiritual impulse in human beings, for the soul's yearning for union with a beloved or a home in the archetypal realm. Our natural longing can lead to ecstatic, numinous experience, communion, and wisdom. Or it can lead to a dark possession, emotional despair, even death. The holy longing is a two-faced archetype, with a light side and a dark side.

In our demythologized world, the holy longing persists in reminding post-modern humanity of another realm, another time, another life. It's like a finger pointing upward to Olympian heights, to our divine mirrors, to our own futures. Or downward to chthonic depths, to Dionysian splendors, to the soul breathing beneath our skin.

The burning of the holy longing brings us into the incandescence of the present moment, into the revelation of light when the veil of darkness parts. Like the burning bush that burns without being consumed, the seeker is alight in rapturous ecstasy.

But sometimes, in the grips of the holy longing, the dream of dissolution may take over. Then, we are infantilized in our helplessness, in the Other's omnipotence. Then, religion is a dark womb.

What is the proper stance toward our holy longing? We might take refuge from it in our rationality, attempting to think away the discomfort of the feeling or rationalize it as an impossible dream. Or we might embrace it with open arms but closed eyes, innocently grasping at teachers or teachings that promise transcendence, while leaving ourselves open to destructive personal or group dynamics. Or we might try to relinquish the desire to go up to spirit and seek only to go down to soul, valuing body over spirit, darkness over light, immanence over transcendence.

Feminists might critique the holy longing for something Other as a sacrifice of individual power, becoming like an object to the divine subject and achieving fulfillment only at the price of autonomy and reason. Certainly, our religious institutions and creeds have been forces for social conservatism, appalling sexism, and even genocide. In fact, they have used our holy longing as currency, promising salvation or higher consciousness in exchange for obedience.

Postmodernists might critique it as a holdover of the modern era when beliefs could simply be believed and egos could simply be taken to have substance. Certainly, our growing capacity to see through beliefs and our growing awareness of the mythic stature of the ego will, in the future, alter the way we describe religious experience.

But I propose that, for many of us, the holy longing carries the seed desire of a life story. If planted deeply enough in the soul, if allowed to gestate, if nurtured carefully, it may yield a rich harvest. Certainly, if one follows the seasons, this seed desire may lead you to the myth at the center of your life, the story that unfolds beneath your yearnings and wanderings.

However, the road is often crooked and narrow: the spiritual dream carries many believers neither into the blue sky of clarity, nor into the waters of absolution; instead it delivers us into the cloud of ambiguity, into the chaos of dissolution. With spiritual shadow-work, I suggest that this very ambiguity can become a way out of the prison of spiritual innocence and into a greater life of spiritual maturity.

To the degree that we do not take our longing into our own souls where it truly belongs and suffer it through as a rite of passage, we will be compelled to live it out literally to the bitter end—and to live only and always in painful longing. But if we can acknowledge our religious yearning and even befriend it, and if we can detect the hidden objects of our desire, perhaps we can follow our holy longing to a higher end.

Invoked or not invoked the gods will be present.

—Oracle at Delphi

Tell me what you yearn for and I shall tell you who you are. We are what we reach for, the idealized image that drives our wandering.

—James Hillman

Whether you follow the ideal of the personal god or the impersonal truth, you will certainly realize the one reality, provided that you experience profound long-ing. The same cake tastes sweet from every direction.

—Ramakrishna

The union of the soul with the light of god, this is what every member of Israel desires with all his heart and all his soul ... to cleave to god and not to be sepa-rated from his blessed unity and oneness.

—*The Tanya*, a Hasidic text

The thing we tell of can never be found by seeking, yet only seekers find it.

—Bayazid Bistami

2

Longing for God: The Hidden Object of Desire

When you imagine god, what do you see? A stern, bearded male perched on a throne with angels circling his head? A beatific madonna seated with an innocent child at her breast? A black, four-armed goddess dancing on a corpse? Indra's net, as it weaves through and interconnects all living beings? The letters of a holy name, a colorful mandala, a sacred mountain, or a sparkling void?

Each organized religion comes with its own images of god full-blown. They may inspire awe, love, fear, guilt, or doubt. They may carry potent and life-restoring energies for a believer, or they may remain lifeless and inert for a skeptic.

According to Genesis, god created human beings in its own image. Therefore, that image is a link between humans and god. Pope John's zealous imitation of saints is an example of the imitation of Christ as the divine image. It's an effort to remove the obstacles that separate lover from beloved in the Christian tradition.

In the Hindu Upanishads, the god images, or *Ishtadevas*, also mediate between the human world and the divine world. The scripture says, "He is, indeed, initiated whose gods within him are initiated, mind by mind, voice by voice."

Islam permits no personified image of god. But the Koran urges believers to repeat without ceasing the name of Allah and to celebrate its praises night and day. In this way, they attempt to awaken and cultivate the attributes of god, as exemplified in its ninety-nine names: mercy, compassion, light, love, sovereignty, holiness, faithfulness, peace.

Buddhism teaches that the Self is an illusion (a no-self or *anatman*); therefore, divine images are illusory. But Tibetan Buddhists use contemplation of a god or goddess as a stage of practice that promises to result in the seeker's transformation into the nature of the divine being. For instance, one contemplates Chenrezig, goddess of compassion, to become more compassionate, green Tara to remove inner obstacles, or Manjusri to sharpen the intellect. In the final stages of practice, however, the images dissolve into emptiness, or non-dual reality.

In Bodhisattva Buddhism, the aspirant moves beyond the ego's longing to avoid suffering and gain happiness and yearns for the happiness of all beings. To achieve this goal, she desires to attain Buddhahood, to be purified from the veil of conflicting emotions and the veil of objects of knowledge. She desires only to be perfected by ultimate knowledge: the union of emptiness and compassion, which is beyond all concepts and images.

At a mythological level, we are what we imagine. The form we give to our divine ancestors in our collective and personal imaginations is the form we aspire to become. So, these images are, in a sense, architectural: we are building our own futures in the world of imagination. When gods are divorced from matter, seekers will disdain their bodies and the earth. When gods are perfect, seekers will strive for purity. When gods are erotic, seekers will see sexual practices as holy. As Episcopal priest Morton Kelsey put it, "The love and celebration of Wotan can produce Hitler and Nazism; the love and celebration of Christos, a St. Francis of Assisi."

If our self-images evolve but our god images do not, they may haunt us like ancestral ghosts. From deep within the unconscious mind, they may sabotage our conscious desires. For example, a transpersonal image of the Bodhisattva, who sacrifices all gain for the enlightenment of humanity, may serve Buddhist monks well. However, for some people with family, economic, and political responsibilities, it may interfere with the needs of a personal life. When one American Buddhist teacher prepared to marry, he found that the inner *imago* of the Bodhisattva kept him from acting on his conscious intentions to build intimate personal attachments, which inevitably involve dependency and suffering.

The ghost of a static god image also may feed feelings of shame and failure. An ex-Catholic woman approaching sixty called me because she could not recover from the shame and guilt she felt about having an abortion in her twenties. Although she no longer consciously believed in the religion of her childhood, unconsciously she carried remnants of the same unforgiving god image, which threatened to punish her for eternity. Like a water lily, that *imago* drew its life force from hidden roots in the waters of the unconscious.

The image of god also evolves in tandem with the image of the archetypal shadow in us. As we imagine the divine, we reject certain traits, which get banished into the demonic. And in this way we disown both the light of the god image and the darkness of Satan. Therefore, if our god images do not evolve, our shadow images remain static as well, narrowing the range in which we can live our conscious lives.

This chapter explores the development of human consciousness through the development of this god image within. These images emerge naturally in the human soul in response to changing circumstances that require distinct symbolic solutions. In contrast to collective symbols of established traditions that are given to us in doctrines or historical events, these images arise spontaneously in our dreams, fantasies, and projections onto other people. And they evolve continuously, offering direct access to the soul, which is not mediated by an institution.

The *imago* is not a conscious image; it's an unconscious symbol, formed by a mix of inner and outer representations of divine figures, beginning with our parents, and our unique temperaments and circumstances. And because it tends to remain hidden from conscious awareness, it carries great charge, often steering the direction of our holy longing.

The spiritual seeker yearns to touch that which is just out of reach or to see that which is just out of sight. In this way, our holy longing points the way toward an image of god, and it, in turn, can guide us in the direction of the ineffable, ungraspable, unknowable realm behind the image.

The Changing God Image: Involution or Down

[Humanity's] helplessness remains and along with it our longing for the father and the gods.

—Freud

At each stage in the growth of human consciousness, the holy longing fuels development via a god image. The changing *imagoes* reflect changing modes of human experience as our holy longing goes through successive stages of projection—from early childhood figures to idealized internal figures to representations of god and, finally, to non-dual reality, in which the images themselves are transcended.

For some individuals, an early image carries symbolic latency: like a seed, it holds a potential for meaning that cannot be fully grasped by childhood awareness. But, with developing consciousness, it yields sweet fruit.

In his autobiography, Jung recounted such a compelling image from his early life. As a child he carved a small man, dressed it in a coat of wood, and set it in a pencil box with a smooth, black stone from the Rhine, which he painted with color. In his imagination, the stone belonged to the wooden man. He hid them in the attic of his home, a secret that gave him a feeling of security for one year.

Many years later, he said, he read about soul-stones in native cultures and realized that he had a clear image of one. The wooden man of his childhood was a little god of the ancient world whose life-force derived from the river stone. To his surprise, he realized that as a child he had spontaneously tapped into archaic levels of the psyche via this potent image. It had captivated him, although its meaning remained unknown for many years.

It's unclear when this process begins. Most psychological theorists discount the possibility of consciousness in the womb or during birth, proposing instead that infants are born with a blank slate and shaped only in their early years. But recent evidence suggests otherwise. At three months, a fetus's five senses operate, its head moves away from lights, it responds to loud noises. In addition, it is stimulated by the mother's heartbeat and digestion. Furthermore, we now know that, through the placenta and the umbilical cord, the fetus is affected by the mother's consumption of food, alcohol, and drugs.

The fetus floats, kicks, sighs, cries, and even does somersaults in its fluid environment. Freud imagined this prenatal sensation of union with mother as the infant's "oceanic feeling." He viewed the later holy longing for mystical union as a childlike wish to re-merge with the mother, a regressive yearning for lost eternity.

Other psychoanalytic thinkers describe this adult fantasy as a wish to have needs met in a perfect relationship that makes no demands. The fantasy may arise in a romantic bond, a therapeutic relationship, or a spiritual liaison. In extreme cases, the individual turns to a world beyond this one for ultimate fulfillment, waiting to be rescued by an idyllic union with an all-loving Other.

But for Freud this mother-longing is not the primary source of the religious impulse. Rather, Freud believed that the origin of the religious attitude can be traced back to an infant's feeling of helplessness and consequent longing for the father's protection.

From two to six months, the infant slips in and out of unconscious unity, or symbiosis. It feels no boundary between itself and the mother's breast. Longing for fusion with the breast, the infant is soothed by it as part of itself. Does the breast carry the *imago* for the sucking infant? It certainly remains a powerful image throughout the life cycle of many men.

Inevitably, the infant's frustration grows because the mother cannot soothe ideally at all times. Much of psychological theory describes the results of unfulfilled longing at certain stages, where development stalls or the individual tries to skip steps. For example, if a man's symbiotic needs were unmet, he may try to get them met as an adult, yearning for an endless supply of love from his wife. But she cannot fulfill his early needs, no matter how nurturing her behavior. Thus his holy longing is displaced onto the wrong object, creating problems in his marriage.

At five or six months, the baby begins to move out of unconscious unity and distinguish between mental images and physical reality. It slowly gains a sense of self, which includes feeling, memory, and bodily awareness. At the same time, it gains a sense of Other—the ideal mother, an *imago* of the perfect soother. In fact, the coherence of the child's growing self-image depends on the presence of an ideal *imago*.

From eight months to two-and-a-half years old, more separation occurs, which we observe in a toddler's persistent drive to walk, despite falling again and again. During this stage, the child comes and goes from the parent, while seeking constancy from her and, at the same time, fearing abandonment. The child may alternate between clinging and rejecting behavior, as he both yearns for reunion with a permanently present *imago* and fears it as well.

Throughout these early stages, the baby's object of longing commonly has maternal qualities. If the infant feels nurtured at the breast, seen and recognized, she will more likely develop a sense of trust that eventually leads to faith and later experiences of transcendence. If she does not, she may feel lost and compensate by constructing a sense of her own omnipotence—a feeling of being *like* god that substitutes for the lost feeling of being *with* god.

(Drawing on the work of anthropologist Jean Gebser, Ken Wilber calls this stage, from ages three to five, magic because, while subject and object are not clearly differentiated, the ego believes it can magically alter the world.)

By age three or four, the child spontaneously imagines a god who is both loving and hating, reliable and inconsistent, much like his mother. The child struggles with separation from the ideal, omnipotent god, just as she struggles with separation from the parent *imago*. She may submit, then rebel, placate, then reject, all the while testing her own powers through magical thinking.

On the other hand, if the mother or other adult severely traumatizes the child and his self fragments, he may fuse with god in a psychotic delusion. One schizophrenic girl whom I treated believed that she was pregnant with Jesus. She had not only become the mother; she was the mother of god.

In the Oedipal stage, from age four and a half until seven, the mother image may be replaced by a representation of the stronger father, who is at once feared and hated, revered and envied. For Freud, this transition is rooted in a boy's sexual desire for his mother and his secret guilt and ambivalence toward his father, whom he wishes to kill. Freud saw this desire acted out on the stage of history when men killed their tribal leaders, from Cronos to Christ, and then idealized them as gods. To appease their guilt, they then performed repetitive rituals to propitiate the father god.

In this way, Freud linked the continual re-shaping of the god image to the ever-changing parent *imago*. As the importance of the parents recedes, their *imagoes* become linked to teachers, heroes, and other authorities, including god.

Feminist researchers have pointed out that Freud's theory doesn't hold for girls because boys' and girls' Oedipal complexes are not symmetrical. A girl does not simply transfer her affection from mother to father and give up her tender feelings for her mother quickly. Instead, the bond is more likely to be sustained, and her relation to her father is added to it. Therefore, girls often come to define themselves more in relation to others, rather than as separate and isolated.

Perhaps, if girls typically remain identified with their mothers and more connected in general, they might be less likely to choose a monastic lifestyle to satisfy their religious longing. They might be more likely to experience the divine in immanent rather than transcendent forms. They might yearn not only for the One impersonal, transcendent god, but for the Many personal, immediate gods.

However, this was not my experience as a masculine-identified girl, or father's daughter. Women like me, who as girls have complex emotional bonds with a dominant father, were not described by Freud and his followers or by feminists today. Some research suggests that father's daughters are often caught in a passive state of waiting for validation, yearning for the impossible: the father's unconditional love, respect, and approval.

Beneath that yearning for the personal father, I suggest that we also long for the archetypal father, the father god, who alone can bestow his blessings. If, later in life, a father's daughter works to reclaim her femininity, this masculine *imago* may become problematic, and the need for a feminine image of god may arise.

Between the ages of seven and ten, the child further distinguishes between god and her parents in the inner world as she faces their human limitations. In this way, god may become all that the parents are not. God may be utterly good and protective, while the parents are neglectful. Or the parents may be loving, while god withholds his gifts. For example, a boy who loves his father but also hates him may isolate his tender longings and place them onto an all-loving god, leaving his father as the object of his hatred. Depending on his religious tradition, he may yearn for god the father and pray to him to intervene in his life. Or he may worship his father, despite his cruelty, and place his hatred onto Satan or another dark *imago*.

(Ken Wilber calls this stage, from ages 6 to 11, mythic because the ego no longer believes it can perform miracles but calls on the gods to intervene through prayer or ritual.)

With the onset of puberty and hormonal changes, a teenager searches for her own identity. She yearns to separate from the family, identify with peers, and find sexual connections outside the family. Often rock stars and celebrities can carry the *imago* for adolescents because their unattainability permits sexual desire to erupt without danger.

In *Myths and Mysteries of Same-Sex Love*, Christine Downing pointed out that Freud located the holy longing in our sexual desire, making of sex itself a god. He saw sexuality as a vehicle through which we express our deepest yearning—our longing to be ourselves and our longing to lose ourselves. So, Downing made the link between the body, the psyche, and the transpersonal realm that Freud resisted making.

During adolescence, a key period for the development of religious images, a teen may abandon the god of her childhood to separate from her parents. If she has a strong intellect, she may judge her faith as childlike and unworthy of an independent adolescent. If her feelings dominate, she may enjoy the music, ritual, or friendship in her religious community and continue to feel close to god in those ways. Or she may attribute to god the ideal qualities of her peers—friendship, loyalty, and an ability to listen. But in any case, her inner *imagoes* continue to be shaped by her outer experience, which in turn is interpreted by her inner world.

Researchers report conflicting *imagoes* during this period, perhaps reflecting our fluid gender roles. For some adolescents, the mother figure is dominant; for others, the same-sex parent is linked to god. In one study, boys emphasized objective, idealized qualities, such as purity and perfection, while girls emphasized emotional qualities, such as love and compassion.

For certain adolescents, a figure of god, such as Christ or Allah, becomes an ideal that, if not tempered, can lead to fanaticism. If a teenager needs to protect a vulnerable self by turning away from human imperfections and merging with a powerful god through religious belief, the seeds of fundamentalism may be planted.

An older female client, who had not resolved her Oedipal issues with her father, entered a cult to recreate that unfulfilled relationship with a charismatic leader. However, she remained stuck in the search for constancy and mirroring from an unavailable father figure when the teacher encouraged devotion and dependency.

(Ken Wilber calls this stage, from age 11 onward, rational because the mind dispenses with myth and tries to understand through evidence.)

From this brief review, we can see that Freud saw the holy longing as a backward pull, a means to express childlike or even infantile needs. For him, religious people are like children trusting a powerful god, who replaced their parents. Freud believed that these needs should be overcome.

More recently, post-Freudian thinkers have expanded on his views, suggesting that the loss of boundaries in an ecstatic mystical state, for instance, may stem from a more advanced stage rather than an early, symbiotic level of development, as Freud would suggest. So, the health of the holy longing depends on our level of development. If we are caught up in primitive defenses, without a fully established ego, the desire to lose ourselves in another person may be a backward, even dangerous wish. But with the achievement of a cohesive ego, it may be a natural impulse to commune with something greater—an evolutionary will to transcend.

In addition, post-Freudians have cited multiple sources of the *imago dei*, insisting that it does not merely reproduce a parental figure. Other researchers measured the similarities between subjects' parental images and god images. They, too, found a complex situation: the image of god was closer to a parental composite than to a single parental image.

W.W. Meissner pointed out that several aspects of a child's developmental experience are relevant for the shaping of an image of god. Early experiences of mirroring by the mother are key. If she is a loving and caring presence, and if the child feels recognized and cherished, he or she will more likely develop a sense of trust and acceptance that allows for religious faith. He also suggested that some aspects of the *imago dei* derive from other significant family members, such as grandparents and siblings, or from cultural models, such as priests or rabbis.

While the holy longing pulls us nostalgically backward, it also pushes us purposefully forward. As early childhood expressions of benevolent or wrathful adults push up from the past and shape a child's image of god, the archetypal dimension calls to us as well, pulling us toward the future, toward reconciliation with the Self, toward higher levels of development.

Unlike Freud, who saw the body and its drives as the vehicle of life, Carl Jung recognized the centrality of spirituality in his patients and in the timeless myths of native cultures. He viewed the religious impulse as a natural part of human life and believed that the unconscious has an authentic religious function, a special directedness toward god. Jung also saw religious issues as foundations of his patients' suffering, which often concealed a deep longing for god, a *Gottesminne* in German.

Jung even attributed purpose to religious experience—an inherent move of the psyche that could be traced not only backward but forward, toward a future goal. That goal, individuation, is expressed by the Self, the transpersonal center of the psyche, which carries meaning, order, and value, and which belongs to the image of god. For Jung, the Self is the ideal *imago,* the dream of totality. It's the beginning of our inner life and the end point toward which we strive.

Jung wrote extensively throughout his 30-year career of the psychological importance of the *imago dei.* He believed that psychic energy creates the god-image by making use of archetypal patterns. As a result, we worship the psychic force within us as something divine.

In his early work, from 1902 to 1911, Jung agreed with Freud that religions were "fantasy systems" designed to resolve sexual problems and that the human-god relationship was rooted in the father-child bond. He saw religion as redirecting the incest wish by spiritualizing it as a relationship to transcendent realities. But, the son of a minister, he believed that individuals were cheated of their own personal relationship to the deity by traditional ethical commandments.

Over the next few years, as Jung studied mythology and began to posit the collective unconscious, he began to lessen his opposition to organized religion, thus weakening his alignment with Freud. In 1920, he referred to a religious attitude as a cultural achievement and to a symbolization of a god image as a great step beyond concrete thinking.

The foundations of Jung's thinking shifted even more as he ceased to identify the god concept exclusively with the Freudian drama of repressed wishes and began to suggest, instead, that it was a symbol of the unconscious itself. Jung soon introduced the term "god-image," saying that, unlike the parent imago, which has an actual point of reference, the *imago dei* corresponds to nothing in the external world and thus cannot be reduced to subjective origins.

From 1921-1949, Jung came to see the contents of the unconscious as "divine" and viewed a direct, overwhelming experience of them as religious experience. In 1937 he adopted from Rudolph Otto the word *numinous* to describe an experience that seizes the individual and overtakes his or her personal will. Drawing from Otto, Jung described the archetype of the god image as having power, mystery, energy, and otherness.

As the concept of the archetypes developed, including the god-image, Jung suggested that, like all projections, it occurred spontaneously. He had become aware of the inadequacy of attempts to explain god-images merely as symptoms of personal problems, ignoring the influence of the collective unconscious. And, as an archetypal symbol, he recognized the god-image as a bearer of meaning.

From 1950 to 1961, Jung revised his thinking about the link between an individual's personal history and his *imago dei*. He no longer saw the child-parent relationship as an adequate model.

During these years, Jung contemplated the opposites contained in symbols, including masculine and feminine, darkness and light. For instance, he saw the image of Christ as expressing the moral tension between conscious and unconscious, good and evil, human and god. But he viewed Christ as perfect, not complete; he would be completed only in relation to his opposite, the Antichrist or Devil. Thus, Jung believed that Christ and Antichrist together represent aspects of a greater totality, the original *imago dei*, which split into opposites in the process of Jesus's human incarnation and later Christian interpretation.

Unlike Freud, who proposed an "education to reality" in order to get over religious thinking, Jung concluded that human beings cannot live without the gods. The destruction of the god-image, he believed, was followed by destruction of the human personality.

Finally, Jung linked the religious imagination to the essence of religious life, claiming that we move in a world of images that point to something ineffable. However, we do not know whether there is something behind these images, which we call god. We know only that, when an individual can survive as a separate person and the ego is stabilized, he or she begins to yearn for something more. For Jung, the holy longing is the ego's yearning to actualize the Self, to open the personal realm to the mythic or archetypal worlds. It's unclear whether he distinguished between the mythic and transpersonal realms. But I believe he conflated the two, unaware all those decades ago of the lived reality of non-dual levels of consciousness.

The Changing God Image: Evolution or Up

All drives are a subset of that Drive, all wants a subset of that Want, all pushes a subset of that Pull—the drive of God toward God … carried out through the intermediary of the human psyche.

—Ken Wilber

Place your devotion whole-heartedly at the service of the ideal most natural to your being. But know with unwavering certainty that all spiritual ideals are expressions of the same supreme presence.

—Ramakrishna

With the rise and consolidation of the ego, the holy longing is transformed from a yearning for individual separateness toward a radiant burning for union with the holy Other. It may emerge as a longing for another individual in romantic union or for a spiritual communion with a group or teacher or for a more unified state of consciousness.

Whatever the object of longing, this is a key turning point in the cycle of consciousness, where involution or "down" into matter meets evolution or "up" into spirit. This latter leg of the journey—from individual back to source—is called the great return among Sufis, *teshuvah* among Jews, and the evolution of consciousness from duality to non-duality among more contemporary mystics and transpersonal thinkers. In the Christian mythos, it signals the end of the incarnation cycle of god becoming human and the burgeoning awareness of Jesus becoming the Christ in the Son/Father unity.

Traditionally, mystics and poets have pointed toward the unknown, unseen, shining source of desire. They ask: What is the dream-like image that calls forth this intense yearning to lose oneself in order to find oneself?

And the sacred traditions have mapped the ascent, which is fueled by the holy longing. They ask: Who am I? What is there on the other side of the veil?

These sacred objects often are imagined in spatial or temporal metaphors: above, below, within, without. Their inherent obscurity is built into our desire for them. The Latin root for the term "desire" is "ceasing to see." For this reason, the holy longing is paradoxical: it involves a blindness, as well as a new kind of sight.

In Wilber's terms, this turning involves the shift from pre-personal to personal (ego) to transpersonal levels of development. Transpersonal experience involves the extension of identity beyond (trans) the individual ego to encompass wider aspects of the mind, humanity, or the cosmos. In the context of transpersonal psychology, the holy longing is an innate urge to transcend the ego, to move up the ladder of evolution, to reach ever greater levels of awareness toward unity with the transcendent One.

In *Sex, Ecology, Spirituality*, Wilber described the four stages of transpersonal development—the psychic, subtle, causal, and non-dual—that complete the great cycle. The psychic level involves an intense union with the material realm and the natural world. For this reason, Wilber refers to it as nature mysticism. But unlike the infant's union with the mother's body, this is a conscious or transpersonal unity, not an unconscious or pre-personal one.

As Wilber put it, individuals at this stage are no longer exclusively identified with the ego. But, because they preserve the ego, the force of the Self can flow through it. And, with the Self, the observing witness arises on a vast expanse of silent awareness and transcends the isolated ego.

This stage is known in the spiritual literature as "cosmic consciousness," the beginning of the end of duality. Absorbed in this stage, the individual transcends the senses, feelings, and thoughts, and tastes union with the divine. He directly apprehends that the Self in him is the same as the Self in every other thing, a common essence. Therefore, the Self of the person and the Self of nature and the Self of culture are one and the same. And the split between subject and object, self and world is overcome.

Wilber pointed out that Ralph Waldo Emerson called this witness the Over-Soul and claimed that it runs through all life. So, when Emerson sang to nature, he actually sang to the Self or spirit that transcends and embraces all life. He was not, as some think, worshipping the natural world alone.

Wilber called this stage the mystical union of matter, life, and culture. It's a result of self-development through self-transcendence; in this case, it's the result of going beyond the ego. And it entails a new ethic: because all sentient beings are expressions of one Self, they should be treated as one's Self. And, as Wilber said, that realization is the source of true compassion, not a moral imperative, but a natural outgrowth of the development of consciousness.

At the subtle level, another, deeper transcendence occurs: nature mysticism gives way to deity mysticism. The Self or spirit that is within and beyond nature, culture, and earth, that is the source and goal of evolution, comes forward. The person experiences subtle sounds and lights, raptures and ecstasies.

It is here that the object of our holy longing, in the form of an *imago dei*, becomes most consciously radiant. St. Teresa of Avila chronicled the rapture, the visions, and the yearning on the way to the establishment of union in the *Interior Castle*. She described her first experience of transcendence with a famous metaphor: the ego, like a worm, emerges as a butterfly in this psychic stage. Then this butterfly yearns for the flame of spirit, in which it is extinguished in the next level of transcendence, the subtle stage.

At this stage, preliminary union is apprehended but not fully established. Teresa says it's like two candles that are joined to give off one light, but can be broken apart again.

In the causal level, this vision is transcended when one is established in the direct experience of union with the divine, which Teresa calls the spiritual marriage. As the ego (worm) died and was reborn as the soul (butterfly), now the soul enters its final union and dies as a separate self—its end point.

We can observe in St. Teresa's evolution how the end point of each stage pulls development in its direction. She establishes a level of consciousness, and the holy longing, which had driven evolution that far, subsides. Slowly, a new force emerges, urging transcendence once more, and her level of consciousness becomes unstable. The soul's holy longing urges her toward the next, higher level of integration, and evolution unfolds toward its end point. At each stage, development proceeds as she transcends and includes each earlier level of consciousness. In this way, each stage finds its fulfillment. And evolution moves toward complete union of the soul with god.

In the causal level, according to Wilber, the soul and spirit, previously united, are now transcended in the prior identity of formless awareness or pure consciousness. That is, the Self *is* spirit, Atman *is* Brahman. The Self is no longer united with spirit but fully identified with it.

In Vedanta, this realization is known as *nirvikalpa samadhi,* which means awareness without any qualities or objects. We can observe it in descriptions of the later years of Ramakrishna's life, as told in Chapter 1.

Meister Eckhart called this experience the naked existence of Godhead. Here the Godhead transcends and includes all worlds. It is, for Eckhart, completely free of all duality and, therefore, "empty," beyond images, concepts, or the witness, beyond intermediaries of any kind.

In this stage of union, the *imago* disappears. As Plotinus put it, "We must not be surprised that that which excites the keenest of longings is without any form, even spiritual form."

Going beyond this identification with formless, boundless, unmanifest spirit, we come to identify with all form. All manifestation appears as a perfect expression of the Self or spirit in the non-dual ground of all stages and dimensions. The Formless and the world of Form are not two, but nondual; not two, but one, as the word *advaita* means.

In Vedanta, this realization is known as *sahaj samadhi,* which means "unbroken and spontaneous so." At this level, nirvana *is* samsara. Brahman *is* the world. Or, as Wilber put it, when all things are nothing but god, there are then no things, and no god, but only *this*. (Wilber's more recent work on stages now elucidates ten levels of consciousness. See his *Integral Spirituality*.)

This, then, is the great cycle of consciousness—the "downward" arc (descent) into individuality and the "upward" arc (ascent) into universality or enlightenment. Although it may appear that spirit is the highest rung on the ladder of evolution, paradoxically, spirit is also the wood out of which the entire ladder and the rungs are made, to use Wilber's metaphor.

In other words, the two aspects of spirit are its transcendental nature and its immanent nature. In this sense, nothing is closer to spirit than anything else. Thus, spirit is the *source* and the course and the goal of all evolution.

The Inner Marriage: A Story of Holy Longing in the Hindu Master Ramakrishna

Ramakrishna, a nineteenth-century Indian saint known as *paramahansa*, or great swan, lived in a garden by the Ganges River near a domed temple dedicated to the goddess Kali—the mother of birth, death, and transformation. Before Ramakrishna's birth, his father had a dream in which the god Vishnu promised to be born as his son. His mother also had a vision of giving birth to a divine child.

When Ramakrishna was a young child, these omens appeared to bear fruit: when the boy portrayed various Hindu gods in religious plays, he lost himself in worshipful contemplation. As he grew, his intensely emotional and devout attitude grew too, and he directed it toward the divine. Eventually, his *bhakti* or devotion opened him to a great yearning for a revelation of Kali, the divine mother. Leaving behind ritual duties, he simply sat before her stone image and sang devotional songs.

According to Lex Hixon in *Great Swan*, in his late teens Ramakrishna had a vision of his *imago dei*: her black form rose out of a golden ocean, with waves rushing at him from all sides. He remained in an ecstatic state for several years, permeated by her radiance, unable to tell day from night. Observers called him the "mad priest of Dakshineswar," but he was mad with divine love.

Ramakrishna reported that for many years, in his painful yearning for god, he was like a bird shrieking for its mate, a kitten mewing for its mother, a cow lowing for its calf. The mention of a divine name would cause his body to catch fire with ecstasy.

He saw himself as a child of Kali, who projects the world from her own essence. And he worshipped her through a young girl in the temple garden, or a passing prostitute, or an advanced practitioner. Later, he dressed in a red sari, and her divine manifestation passed through his form—he became her. All separation dissolved.

In the dawn light, the scent of incense filling the air, Ramakrishna bowed before a black basalt image of Kali that was adorned with colorful flowers, while chanting in Bengali the names of god. Then he sat on a white cloth, half-naked and chewing spices, and welcomed his visitors as messengers of his beloved. They bowed and touched their foreheads to the floor on entering.

Ramakrishna spoke of the path and goal of the mystic way: passionate immersion in god. Suddenly, this all-embracing love of which he spoke overtook him, and he urged his disciples to cry to the Lord with an intensely yearning heart. Too many people shed tears for their children; they shed tears for money, he said. Instead, cry to the Lord.

He likened our longing to the rosy dawn. After the dawn the sun comes out. Longing is followed by a vision of god, he said. Then his eyes rolled up, his breath stilled, and he disappeared into a state of absorption.

Ramakrishna sought to experience the divine presence through all sacred traditions, so he did practices from Tantra, Vedanta, Islam, and Christianity. Eventually he could embody the holy figures of these religions and transmit their energies through his own form. In this way, he expressed and transcended the gods and goddesses and merged into the greater spirit.

For example, when he practiced remembrance of the name of Allah and became absorbed in it, he had a vision in which the Prophet Mohammed's radiant form blended with his own. When he concentrated on Christ, he merged with the divine form of Jesus.

A visitor belittled Ramakrishna's god images as figments of the imagination. The holy man responded by asking the visitor to consider the yearning of those who follow this path: it's like the attraction between lovers who long to meet and merge. More than that, it's like the divine lovers Radha and Krishna, for whom this burning attraction is infinite. Those practitioners who commune with the divine through sacred icons shed tears of longing to be able to penetrate the outer forms of wood, stone, or clay, he said. They long to experience divine reality directly. We can echo their cry and ignore the images they worship, he said. This is another path to god-realization.

Eventually, Ramakrishna cut through his own personal image of the divine, the goddess Kali. Her form dissolved, and his self disappeared into her formlessness. For three days he sat in a high level of *samadhi*, united with god.

When his wife asked him not to remain in the formlessness of bliss but to return to the edge of individuality, he learned to operate in that gap between the pure consciousness of *samadhi* and the waking state. He moved in and out of the open sky of unity, impervious to duality.

Ramakrishna reportedly once said that young men and women who long for god from childhood are divine in human form. They are god nakedly longing for god.

During both involution and evolution, the *imago* calls to us. It is the lure to consciousness. Whether the archetype is disguised in the clothing of the mother who cannot be won, or the beloved who cannot be possessed, or the home that cannot be found, it is ours to continually approach, to approximate, to yearn for.

For many years, I have wondered why the theme of exile recurs in religious history. Today I see exile as a symbol for the separation from the divine, specifically from our images of god. During these fallow periods of exile, the holy longing of a people for a homeland and a new *imago* can be intense. With the destruction of the first Jewish temple in Jerusalem and the exile in Babylonia, the tribal deity of the Jews was transformed. Bishop John Spong has suggested that the Christian community is undergoing a similar ordeal today: exile from an outdated Church and yearning for an updated image of god.

Likewise, for an individual, the separation from an *imago,* because it no longer holds holiness or serves the soul, leaves one feeling like a refugee in exile. When the Sufi poet Rumi could no longer gaze upon the face of his beloved teacher, which had become for him the face of god, he wandered aimlessly in a desert of thirst until he attained a new level of consciousness.

I had a similar experience: when the *imago* of the self-realized yogi became tarnished for me, I felt compelled to leave my spiritual community to maintain my integrity. I felt lost and alone, a homeless wanderer without direction or companionship until, eventually, a fresh *imago* emerged.

Therefore, as we develop, our image of the divine must evolve as well. If it remains all-powerful, we may remain feeling childlike. If it remains all-knowing, we may remain feeling ignorant. If we imagine a formless god, one that is not a being but a state of being, we may remain feeling inadequate and unenlightened, striving to attain the unattainable.

Today, at the height of the ego's reign, many people believe we have outgrown the gods. They can be explained away as projections or reduced to childhood fantasies. But I believe, with Jung, that the archetype of god incarnates within us as the Self, a spark of the divine. And it will be present, called or uncalled.

If the *imago* remains unconscious, if it acts upon us outside the boundaries of awareness, then it can pull us like a magnet toward unknown territory. It can keep the heart in bondage to childhood representations. It can trap the mind in idolatry. It can cause the soul to wander endlessly, without rest.

With our overemphasis on rationality, the holy longing has been banished. In turn, this has resulted in the widespread loss of the *imago dei*. However, just as building a relationship to our shadow images can deepen and enrich our soul life, so can the meeting with the god image. And in our society that encounter often takes place when we fall in love.

Who is it we spend our entire life loving?

—Kabir (trans. by Robert Bly)

Who is your double in the extended realm of the soul? Who or what is it that is yearning for you, calling to you; who is the Beloved you are always trying to remember?

—Jean Houston

I tasted you and I now hunger and thirst for you; You touched me, and I have burned for your peace.

—St. Augustine

The only beloved is the living mystery itself.

—Kathleen Raine

What is behind all this desirousness? A thirsting for the eternal.... desire only burns in order to burn itself out, and in and from this fire arises the true living spirit which generates life according to its own laws.

—C.G. Jung

3

Longing for the Human Beloved: The Search for Romantic Union

Like a moth longing for the flame, insane for the light that will extinguish its very life, the lover longs for the beloved partner. To further paraphrase the Goethe poem cited in Chapter 1: As long as you have not experienced this, to lose yourself in another, you are only a guest on this earth.

This chapter examines the holy longing in the context of romantic love. In many relationships, one person is like a moth—which yearns to dissolve boundaries and melt in ecstatic union. The other is like a flame—which burns brightly on its own. The first person suffers terribly with separation, sensing even the slightest rejection as abandonment or loss. The second person suffers terribly with fears of being smothered or snuffed out, as if the partner could extinguish her light.

What is the relationship between this longing for a human beloved, or *imago amore*, and the longing for the divine beloved, or *imago dei?*

The Greek god of desire, Eros, helps us to imagine our human desire as a divine power by giving it the name of a god. This naming honors the awesomeness of our experience of it. The ego cannot willfully direct our desire; it directs us. We cannot make ourselves desire one object over another; the objects of our desire choose us. We cannot even make ourselves stop desiring an object. Therefore, we are subject to it, as we are subject to a god.

Eros appears on the threshold between our reach and our grasp, drawing a thin line between subject and object, lover and beloved, and thereby stoking the fires of holy longing. We glimpse the beloved, and walls of separation crumble. We gaze into his eyes and recognize an ancient symmetry. We hear an obscure call to ascend, to leave our limitations behind in a flight toward the heavens. An instant later, we are jolted back to earth, inside our own skin, inside our own solitude, inside our own suffering.

The god Eros lives in this gap between what we have and what we seek, what we are and what we are becoming. He turns the object of our projection into the numinous Other, forever present, forever unattainable.

This god points to the root of human nature as desiring and longing. He speaks to an urge that is more fundamental than a desire for a person or a thing. I suggest that it's not people we crave; it's not sexual union; it's not material satisfaction. It's self-transcendence toward a higher level of spirit, toward union with god.

And Eros *is* that driving force in the cosmos. Eros is the holy longing of the human for the divine, the longing of the one for the holy Other. And when it appears in the form of romantic yearning, it is ultimately a spiritual desire for greater and greater union or completion.

Therefore, the erotic yearning of human love both conceals and reveals divine love. It is not simply individual longing; it contains or reflects cosmic longing. Within or behind the person we love, we seek an object of worship, an *imago amore*, a means to connect to the divine.

So, the purpose of love is not what it seems: it is not merely about forming partnership and family for love and security. Rather, its inner purpose is to evoke an image of the long lost beloved, whose call initiates an unpredictable and sometimes painful journey back to the Self.

This motif has appeared many times in human history and legend. Between the eleventh and thirteenth centuries, the Christian tradition of courtly love emerged, in which knights and troubadours pined with ardent longing for married women. The woman's amiable smile charmed them; her gentle voice seemed celestial; her eyes shone like jewels. The knights felt their ardor from a distance and held the beloved's image in their hearts.

Because the object of their desires was unattainable, the knights' love could be spiritualized, their devotion refined and perfected. They submitted to the wound of unrequited longing, asking nothing of the beloved, and in this way their desires were purified of ego. They praised her and served her selflessly, cultivating the Christian virtues of patience, fidelity, humility, and faith. And internally, in an exchange of hearts, they united with her, resting their heads on her breast, just as St. John rested on Christ's.

In this context, the lady, the *imago amore*, stood in for something greater, something more transcendent, a mirror of the divine beloved. Therefore, she came to be called a "mystical queen." The knight's devotion to her prepared his heart for higher devotion. The aim of troubadour love was not to marry; it was to prepare the soul for union with god.

The same point can be made about Dante: he first glimpsed Beatrice when she was eight years old, and he was nine. Nonetheless, he claimed that, from that moment, love would govern his soul. Although each of them married another, Dante cherished Beatrice's *imago* and, eventually, it enabled him to ascend in the *Paradiso* toward divine love.

I confess that I, too, suffered the same rapture and torment as a young girl. When I first saw Steve, I knew, in my tiny heart, that one life ended and another began. When I watched him across the schoolyard, an inexplicable, wistful yearning descended on me. He seemed perfect, shining, godlike. Yet he was just out of reach. When, for brief moments, we spoke or danced together, I grew wings.

My parents became worried. Such an intense infatuation at such a young age seemed unnatural. They wanted to rescue me or fix me. But my longing only grew stronger. I was not content to contemplate his beauty from afar. I imagined that Steve and I would marry one day, and this terrible yearning would end when I shared life with him. No other images of union were available to me.

As the winds of life swept us apart through the years of middle school and high school, I continued to watch him, just out of reach across the classroom or the schoolyard. His blond curls, his freckled nose, his blue eyes haunted me. Until one night, lying on my back and reaching up to the heavens, I called out for help—and all of the radiant burning that had been directed toward Steve suddenly changed direction: I yearned for god.

The wrenching cessation of my romantic longing was the poignant beginning of my spiritual life. When I saw Steve the next day and the day after that, I still beheld a vision of beauty. I still felt the pain of separation from him. But something larger stirred in my heart. I began to see it through him, not merely in him.

When college took me out of town, I still carried his image tenderly within me. But other images of the beloved began to appear. And when his life took a tragic turn and he was taken away finally and forever, I still loved that boy in the man fiercely. But I came to feel, as Dante did, that what I had fallen in love with at such a tender age was not Steve, but the divine beloved, the *imago amore* that lived in him.

Today I feel deep gratitude to the boy and to the divine image that he carried for me. Together they prepared my soul to love god and awakened in me the holy longing, the yearning that still stirs today and leads me to this moment in which I write these words.

Therefore, rather than focus on how to achieve a love union in daily life, which is a widespread preoccupation in our romance-obsessed culture, this chapter explores the separation that is inherent in any union, the impossibility of possessing the beloved. For those who feel they cannot find a worthy partner, the separation is all they know. Longing to be cherished, even ennobled in the eyes of a loved one, they may devalue their accomplishments and their other relationships, which seem meaningless unless they are shared with that special person.

For those who have known the beloved and lost him or her, either through abandonment or death, the separation can be acute and consuming. If they believe that the object of their desire has been present and is then absent, their desire burns. Praying fervently for the return of the beloved who can grant fulfillment, they may feel that nothing else can quench this thirst.

And for those who are graced to share daily life with the beloved, separation is also ever-present. It is suffered in the very nature of our closeness and our distance, our sameness and our otherness. We sense it as we feel the press of skin on skin but cannot go deeper into one another. We know it as we hit the wall of a different opinion or the fortress of a separate reality but cannot find common ground. We intuit it as we watch our lives unfold in different directions, as if we follow two parallel paths that can never meet. In the end, we understand what the poet Rainer Maria Rilke meant when he said that love is two solitudes watching over one another.

Finally, for those who yearn for the divine child to redeem them from their own choices and limitations, separation is poignant. No matter how we cling, from the beginning it's evident that a child has a temperament and fate of its own.

Psychologically, we might say that consciousness grows through cycles of union and separation, through seeing the difference between ego and Other and transcending that difference. But separation can be a dark passage, accompanied by a painful yearning to return, to reconnect again with the source.

I suggest that, despite inherent separation, an image of the beloved can be accessed through an individual soul's desire. And, like the *imago dei,* the *imago amore* evolves as our consciousness develops. Therefore, as the tension of otherness ignites our yearning, love becomes a vehicle of evolution.

Beloved as parent: the psychology of love

Behind the search for the magical Other lies the archetypal power of the parent *imagoes.* Our first experience of ourselves is in relationship to these primal Others.

—James Hollis

We are conceived in desire. Our mouths salivate with desire. Our genitals burn with desire. Our hands grasp with desire. Our eyes gaze with desire. We yearn to melt into the beloved, to find our other half, and to lose ourselves in eternal union.

The romantic search today has taken on religious proportions. We long for the ideal partner, the beloved Other, as we long for god, the holy Other. It is in our intimate lives and our spiritual lives that we are most likely to meet the Self or *imago dei*. It is also in our relationships and our religions that we become most wounded and disillusioned.

Perhaps this occurs because, inevitably, we bring our early emotional unmet needs to a romantic union. Hidden within our erotic yearnings lie child-like yearnings—the desire to return to a lost garden of innocence, the longing for unconditional love and acceptance, the wish to depend on someone else to satisfy our needs. When we meet a potential partner and fall in love, all of these hopes are activated and, with them, an intense yearning to merge arises in our souls.

If we long to merge with a mother or father *imago* in a symbiotic union, we recreate the early, unconscious bond with a parent. For this reason, we unknowingly attribute highly positive traits to our partners and imagine that they will be the perfect parents, fulfilling the ideal parent *imago* in the exact ways that our own parents did not. For example, a young man imagines that his girlfriend always will be emotionally available and nurturing, unlike his absent mother. A girl imagines that her boyfriend always will be kind and supportive, unlike her critical and controlling father. This is a natural and inevitable process of projection, which allows the unconscious bond to form between two lovers and feels to them like a mysterious alliance, an echo of the past.

These fantasy images of the beloved—generous, pure, kind, selfless, controlling, abandoning, cruel—are, in part, made up of familiar parental qualities. When we feel a harmonic match with another person, a familiar resonance, we reawaken to our soul's dream of union, and we recreate early childhood patterns of loving and wounding.

These projections may take on mythic proportions, as we imagine that a boyfriend is a hero or savior whose qualities will save rescue us from the limitations of our parents. When one of my clients was an infant, her father died of tuberculosis. And as she grew, the secret promise of his love grew too. That promise became an emptiness inside her, a hunger for love or, more accurately, for union with the ghost of her father—an impossible union.

She soon found unavailable men to stoke the fires of her longing—married men, gay men, and other inappropriate partners for her. She believed that if she bonded with an available man her yearning would cease. Then who would she become? This unknown self terrified her, so she chose the yearning over a loving relationship.

Eventually, she projected her longing onto spiritual teachers, but the emptiness remained. One would feed her mind for a while; another would receive her devotion. But, in the end, their human flaws became apparent, and they fell from grace, shattering her ideal *imago*. She cried out in grief and rage at them, but they were just limited human beings, she told me. God was really to blame.

Slowly, this dream of union with her lost father/god loosened its grip. No human on the outside, no image on the inside could fill her up. She was thrown back on herself, on her own resources, on her own feelings. Eventually, she began to permit herself to feel the yearning without trying to fix it. She began to turn within rather than to external saviors. She practiced yoga daily, wrote in her journal each morning, and found words and images to tell the tale of her anxious restlessness, her wistful yearning. Gradually, the psychic energy that she had been giving away all those years began to return home.

Jungian analyst Marion Woodman calls this archetypal pattern the ghostly lover. She tells the story of poet Emily Dickinson, who shared her father's pursuits and standards of perfection. In fact, she lived to please her father. As Woodman put it, he controlled her soul.

Unconsciously bound to a father/god, Dickinson fell in love with an unavailable man and projected her parent *imago* onto him. In her fantasy, she lived in a world that could never be, a life removed from reality. And she remained a child in her father's house, a maiden in white writing poems.

Although we are grateful today that Dickinson was able to turn her suffering into art, we feel dismay if we consider her actual life. Cut off from her bodily instincts and her capacity to develop a feminine maturity, instead she worshipped an *imago* from afar and displaced her passion onto the page. Confined by her cultural moment, unable to rebel or to live out her own life, she raged at god, who demanded her suffering and withheld her happiness.

In some cases, the yearning for an unavailable lover may involve an Oedipal *imago*, an adolescent desire for the opposite-sex parent who is bonded to someone else. These triangles are evident in marital affairs, in which one dreams of killing off the same-sex spouse in order to win the other for oneself. And they are evident in family systems, in which a child intervenes between the parents and takes over the energy and attention of one of them.

The romantic longing due to separation also may occur when a parent was physically present but emotionally absent, as in a couple in their twenties who came for marital therapy. The young man, who was initially drawn to his wife's independence, now suffers terribly when she pulls away to work, spend time with friends, or defend herself against his neediness. He feels neglected and abandoned, as he did as a child when his emotionally unavailable mother left him with a nanny each day to return to work. In order to fend off intense feelings of abandonment and loneliness, he seeks to merge with his beloved through sexual intimacy. But these moments of pre-personal union are never enough to fill the emptiness.

Ever watchful for his wife's psychic or emotional withdrawal, he demands that she open up more deeply and offer more nurturing. He seduces her into sexual contact more frequently than she wants, and he criticizes her for being distant and uncaring in a frenzied attempt to uphold his parent *imago*.

The result: she feels trapped, controlled, and inadequate as a partner. Somehow, she can never get it quite right for him. Remarkably, she felt the same way as a child in the face of her demanding alcoholic father. Powerless when confronted by his mood swings and constant criticism, she learned to placate him, to try to care for his needs, and to withdraw when she failed. So, in her marriage, she yearns for separateness, time alone to daydream and to feel free of control and caretaking.

While the husband—projecting his mother *imago*—needs more relatedness and feels traumatized with abandonment when he doesn't receive it, she projects her father *imago* and feels traumatized with engulfment, as if she will be devoured. He draws close to her flame; she sputters, fearing she will be snuffed out. As a result, they develop strategies to manage their anxiety and to attempt to heal their own childhood wounds. But they end up in chronic crises around their respective unmet needs, while they simultaneously re-wound each other in repeating patterns. Unable to hold the tension between separateness and union, eventually they become resentful and hopeless. Or one of them seeks to regain the promise of romance through an affair.

To many people in relationships, this opposition appears to be a power struggle between two sets of needs, both conscious and unconscious. However, beneath a negotiation for time together and time apart, emotional union and emotional separateness, there lies a deeper impulse: the yearning for self-transcendence through a series of projections and disappointments, which constitutes the nature of every intense loving relationship.

If the partners work with their own *imagoes* and withdraw their projections, their relationship may move through the levels of consciousness: from symbiotic to magic to mythic to rational to transpersonal. At the rational stage, an adult relationship emerges, in which each person has a consolidated ego that is independent enough to relate to the other through rational negotiation of differences. In these marriages, the partners experience their separateness (or union) as acceptable and join together for reasons of compatibility to achieve tasks. They may be able to bypass difficult unconscious emotional material and function well together. But they often report that although their union is harmonious, it's not juicy. It's lacking a spiritual foundation.

Ideally, this personal or rational level of development can become a platform for transpersonal growth. In this way, human love promises to initiate us into divine love.

Beloved as god: the archetypes of love

Every lover is fain that his beloved should be of a nature like to his own god … his every act is aimed at bringing the beloved to be like unto himself and unto the god of their worship.

—Plato's *Phaedrus*

A man who identifies with his own ideal … can't accept that the white radiance of his beloved can be stained by the humanity of her own excremental functions.

—Marion Woodman

Clearly, the parent *imago* is not the sole hidden object of our desire when we fall in love. On a deeper level, the search for the romantic beloved is a spiritual search, an attempt to return not merely to the oceanic feeling but to conscious, ecstatic union with the divine. This process takes place via the projection of the Self onto the idealized Other, who becomes soul mate, hero, goddess, savior. As a result, the *imago amore* appears to reside in the beloved, and the lover yearns for union with him or her.

In a case history of holy longing for the romantic beloved, Jung explored the written fantasies and poems of a young American woman named "Miss Miller." While traveling from New York to Europe, she spent long hours writing poetry in a dream-like state on a ship's deck. When she caught a glimpse of a handsome officer on deck for the night-watch, his image opened a new world to the girl, a world of erotic yearning.

Jung suggested that Miss Miller had to bury her sexual feelings and, to avoid that inner conflict, unconsciously wrote a hymn to a masculine god, thereby replacing earthly love with heavenly love. Following her vision of the man, she wrote a poem, "The Moth to the Sun," describing her glimpse of the beloved and her resulting longing which, like the moth's, could end only in a rapturous death.

Jung pointed out that her hopeful tone could not be sustained because the longing returned again and again. Her hope was in vain, Jung said, because she was a mortal who was momentarily borne up on the wings of her longing into the light—and then sank down again to death.

But I suggest that disappointment and loss are inevitable in intense romantic relationships even when they are consummated in intimacy and marriage. During romance, the Self is activated, and we feel special, purposeful, and even exalted. The beloved seems to be divine because he provides access to the qualities of the Self, or *imago amore.*

But we cannot possess that moment; we cannot control it, for it is larger than us. It is not personal, but archetypal. So, when a partner disappoints us or betrays us, which is inevitable, the projection of the Self rattles. The guardian of the *imago* fails us in some way, and we feel emptiness and despair.

If we unconsciously believe that the Other is responsible for our experience of meaning and purpose, then we may try to coerce his or her words and actions to meet our needs. For a moment, a woman may carry the *imago* again for her husband, and he may feel his fragmented self cohere with meaning and worthiness. But, in the next moment, she fails him again, and he rages against the loss. So, he will try to get her to behave once more in ways that rebuild the projection and maintain his *imago.*

However, in this process he will not see her as she is. And she will feel used and controlled. Eventually, she may feel resentful and become unwilling to provide the Self for him.

Thus the risks for the lover are great: the one who projects the ideal suffers diminishment and loss, identifying with the inferior, unworthy position in a relationship. And in giving away the light, he fails to know it in himself. He may suffer terrible cycles of gain and loss, happiness and despair, while continuing to believe that his partner is responsible for these swings.

In addition, if he projects power and knowledge onto his partner, he may sacrifice his own authority and silence his own voice. In extreme cases, he may become a hostage to love, believing that he can survive only when the relationship is enacted in specific ways.

And the risks for the beloved are also high: those who carry the ideal Self for another may suffer under its weight. Unconsciously, they may feel the pressure to live out their partner's ideal *imago*, rather than live an authentic life. One woman, seen by her boyfriend as a goddess, told me that she felt idolized, not loved; she felt objectified, not seen. Also, an individual who is the target of these spiritual projections may get snared in identifying with them and become inflated, feeling himself to be special or powerful, which may lead to narcissistic abusive behavior.

Those inner and outer figures who carry the Self or *imago amore* for others can appear via many archetypal images. They are shaped by our parent *imagoes*, the symbolic landscape of our play, the intellectual landscape of our education, and cultural messages about masculine and feminine beauty. If we feel needy or help-less and long to be saved or rescued, we may be attracted to the lover who appears as hero or savior. If we feel flawed and long for healing, we may be drawn to the lover who appears as healer. If we feel dry or over-controlled and long for erotic passion, we may be drawn to the lover who appears as a wild, unrestrained Dionysus or Aphrodite or to a playful divine child. If we feel insecure and yearn for approval, we may be attracted to the lover who appears as a good mother or father, teacher or mentor.

In her book *In Search of a Woman's Passionate Soul,* Caitlin Matthews described the development of the inner image of her own masculine ideal. In early childhood, she played with invisible companions who were feminine. But with the onset of menstruation and her body's transition into womanhood, the inner figure became masculine, primarily a swashbuckling pirate who performed daring deeds on the high seas. Matthews attributed her early marriage to a man who lived outside the margins of society to the influence of this inner masculine ideal. Later, the inner masculine figure became an ancient Irish poet, who guides her creative life to this day.

A male client recalled feeling his longing aroused at an all-boys college when he studied Renaissance humanists and poets. The world of imagination opened to him and a current ran through his body. At night, he peered up at the starry sky and called out to his poet-heroes, "Where are you?" He hoped that these eter-nal spirits would be his companions in the realm of creative imagination.

In this man's third year at college, women were permitted to attend for the first time. He remembered one co-ed in particular whose large breasts captivated him. From that moment, his longing became eroticized and directed toward the feminine ideal.

During a period of career building and marriage, he said, his holy longing was dormant, the fire banked. But, later, when he met a woman whose life was dedicated to exploring creativity and consciousness, his longing burst into flame. Suddenly, he yearned for the freedom, openness, and creative potential that she represented for him. When he was with her, he felt alive, optimistic, and imaginative.

As long as this woman carried the feminine ideal for him, he felt liberated by her. His masculinity awakened at a deeper level and, at the same time, his hunger for the spiritual dimension increased. But when, through psychedelics and later through meditation, he began to have a direct experience of the Self, his reliance on her lessened. Instead of the woman acting as his guide to the soul, his own inner ideal became his guide.

Another woman client, who was less interested in mating than most, met the *imago* in a series of male friends. In college, she felt a platonic partnership with a man who set her on the back of his motorcycle and took her away from academic life on wild adventures. Later, she formed a deep spiritual friendship with a man who matched her intellectual gifts and became like a member of her family. In her forties, she befriended another man with whom she lived, as brother and sister, for several years. For her, the soul brother carried the *imago*.

In whatever image it appears, the romantic beloved brings a meeting with the Other. And because of its autonomy, it often brings suffering, lack of control, and lack of certainty. The very safety that we may have sought in a relationship remains elusive. But the inner marriage awaits.

The inner marriage: A story of holy longing in the Sufi lovers Majnun and Layla

In Sufism, the love-mad religion, there is a famous tale, which is recalled to this day in the poems and songs of many peoples. In it we can glimpse the possibility that love brings self-transcendence, even union with the divine—the inner marriage.

As told by twelfth-century Persian poet Nizami, a Bedouin noble man had satisfied all of his desires but one: he had no son in whose memory he would live on. As he grew older, his yearning for a son grew greater. Yet for many years his prayers and alms were in vain.

Then, late in life, the man's wife gave birth to a boy, whose jewel shone through the veil of his body. They called him Qays, and he became as tall and slender as a cypress.

When he was a young boy, a girl joined his class at school—and Qays' heart filled with longing at the sight of her. Layla's face was a lamp beneath the dark shadow of her hair. Her eyes, like a gazelle's, her lips, like roses. She, too, drank the potion and became drunk on the sight of her beloved.

Intoxicated with one another, they turned away from the world; but the world turned toward them, taunting them with judgment and jealousy. Qays' mind urged him to avoid Layla, but his heart was torn with desire for her. Togetherness was dangerous; separation was torture.

Layla's tribe tried to protect her honor: they guarded her at home, where she hid the sorrow in her heart.

Unable to see her, Qays roamed about like a sleepwalker, stumbling and falling. He wandered aimlessly in small alleys between the tents and among the stalls in the bazaar, where merchants sold food and spices. He sang melancholy songs, lamenting his lost love, as tears flowed down his cheeks. He lost not only his beloved; he lost himself.

The people said, "He is a *majnun*, a madman." And the more they called him that, the more he became Majnun, until his vain hopes chased him out into the desert, barefoot and bareheaded. All at once, under a blue tent of sky, verses poured out of his mouth—a message for Layla to be carried on the east wind. "Invisible candle, do not torment the moth fluttering around you. My longing is my heart's consolation, its wound and its healing balm."

At night, when others slept, he snuck back to the tribe and kissed the threshold of Layla's tent. He crawled away again before the first light, escaping her in order to find her.

Empty-handed, his coarse robe torn to shreds from top to bottom, his hair matted about his face, he roamed the deserts aimlessly. And as he wandered, he composed verses and called out her name—Layla, Layla—again and again, like chanting the name of god. All other desires burned away but the desire for union with her. All other images dissolved but the image of her lovely face, the face of his beloved. She was a rosebush; he watered it with his tears.

Majnun's father made the pilgrimage to Mecca to pray for his son, to no avail. He traveled into the mountains to find him and pleaded with him to come home and find pleasure there. But the son replied that he did not choose his fate; it chose him, and he was caught in its noose.

In the meantime, Layla became lovelier to those who saw her. But she saw only Majnun; her eyes formed only the image of him.

One afternoon in the bazaar, a child was singing the verses of Majnun, like a nightingale in spring. Soon, every wanderer was singing his songs and bringing them to the people. Layla could hear the voice of her lover in their voices. She wrote down the verses on scraps of paper and entrusted them to the wind. When someone found one of them, he carried it to Majnun with the hope of hearing a response. The beloved answered at once, the messenger memorized the verse and, on returning, delivered it to Layla.

Troubled by the madman's raving and the attention he drew to their daughter, Layla's parents made plans to marry her to another. Sitting in a litter carried by camels, bedecked like a princess, she made the journey from her tribe's tents to her husband's. But that night, when he tried to enter her garden, Layla told him that she was sworn to another man and would never share his bed. While the husband's eyes searched for Layla, hers looked only for Majnun.

Majnun's life became nothing but longing for Her. All other desires burned away in the flame that was desire for Her. He became detached from the things of this world—the pleasures, the sorrows, the comforts, the pains. As the Sufis say, he ate the eater in himself.

In the dark of night, Majnun cried out his prayers to the glittering stars. When a deep calm arrived, he slept and dreamed of a tree growing out of the ground to great heights in front of him. When he looked up, he saw a bird fluttering through the leaves toward him. Something glittered in its beak. The bird let it drop onto the crown of Majnun's head. It was a jewel.

On awakening, Majnun was flooded with happiness. His body felt as if it could fly. His soul had wings. He leapt into the air, turning.

The next day, several people observed scraps of paper flying about with the two names, Majnun and Layla, written upon them. Passing a tent, Majnun reached out and caught a bit of paper with "Layla" in his fist—then tore it to bits.

"Why did you tear up the paper?" a woman veiled in black asked the boy.

"Because one name is enough for us. You have only to scratch me, and out falls Layla."

"But why did you throw away her name and keep your own?" the woman persisted.

"You can see the shell but not the kernel," said the boy, as he spread his arms and looked down upon his rags. "The name is the outer shell, me. But the face beneath is Hers."

Majnun vanished, becoming nothing but the beloved.

With the collapse of projections onto our romantic beloveds, the real work begins. He is not the ideal father; she is not the feminine goddess. Our partners, so idealized and divine in one moment, so flawed and human the next, cannot carry the weight of our *imagoes*. We cannot return to the garden through them. And we must not blame them for this failure.

Rather, we can see through our projections to the authentic Otherness of our partners—their distinct needs, wounds, preferences, and sensibilities. We can bear witness to their light and to their shadows. At first, the discrepancy between who they actually are and who we thought they were may be startling and painful. All we can see is what the Other is *not*: not nurturing, not available, not creative, not heroic. Definitely not unconditional.

At this stage, some relationships break down and divorce ensues. We cannot tolerate the inherent separateness of the Other, so we repudiate it and literalize separateness. For other couples, psychic and emotional separation occurs, which may speed one or both partner's development out of symbiotic union or magical thinking and toward autonomy.

Slowly, we come to see that our beloved partner is not responsible for carrying our ideal *imago*. She cannot be the all-nurturing mother or the divine goddess indefinitely. He cannot be the all-giving father or the daring hero without human flaws. Eventually, we can recognize that what they carried for us was inside of us all along. What we see in the beloved is an aspect of ourselves, whether it is the ideal parent or the ideal Self. As we begin to reclaim it, we enlarge our own souls.

For example, the longing partner can begin to cultivate more autonomy and learn to provide for her own needs; the independent partner can begin to cultivate more dependency and learn to feel safe with intimacy. As the two extend into their disowned patterns, they can open to feeling a deep empathic bond for the other.

When we carry our own wounds and our own greatness, we need our loved ones in a different way. Instead of requiring them to parent us or to mirror a disowned part of ourselves, we can love them more as they are, with conscious devotion rather than unconscious need. In this way, we give up our demands on our partners to provide us with an ideal Self. And instead we can choose consciously to meet each other's needs, rather than feel unconsciously driven to meet them out of fear.

As we struggle to reclaim projections and maintain responsibility for fulfilling our own needs, a deeper purpose of a loving relationship becomes more clear: it's a container in which to cultivate interdependence, the dance between love and freedom, union and autonomy.

Eventually, our holy longing for a higher union arises again. The end point of psychological development, a consolidated ego, is not enough. Our yearning for the *imago* in a human beloved guides us on, transforming Eros from its conventional association with erotic union toward a desire for spiritual union.

To return to Ken Wilber's levels of consciousness: the first stage of love beyond the ego is psychic, in which we transcend the otherness of the beloved and perceive the same Self in him or her as we witness in ourselves. This taste of spiritual union is a taste of transpersonal love.

Today lovers may catch a glimpse of the Self in the Other when they meditate together, staring into one another's eyes. Or they may tune into it if they take psychedelics together, especially MDMA or Ecstasy, which appears to melt individual boundaries and open us to this level of union. However, many seekers report that this experience, while profound, is not the basis for a functioning relationship. A glimpse of the Other's deeper nature does not imply compatible personalities, values, or lifestyles.

At the subtle level, we yearn to transcend even that distinction of the Self, like the butterfly being extinguished in the flame. Like practitioners of Tantra, we use the image of the beloved as the image of the divine, a doorway beyond form, beyond attachment, to a higher transcendence.

Finally, at the causal level, a rare attainment in human beings, the *imago* disappears altogether, and the soul dies to any sense of separateness, in unity with the divine.

Our yearning for the romantic beloved, then, is not merely rooted in the search for approval or the desire for sex. It is a part of Eros, a larger cosmic longing with which the whole of life pulses. Its intention is to awaken us to a prior connection with all life via the connection to one human being. In this way, the beloved serves again as a window onto the divine.

Whoever travels without a guide needs two hundreds years for a two-day journey.

—Rumi

You must long for the guru like a flower opening to receive the rain, flock to the guru for refuge like birds seeking shelter from a storm. You should pray to accompany the guru through all your lives like a body and its shadow, not separate for even an instant.

—Stephen Butterfield

When Buddhist meditation teacher Jack Kornfield complained to his abbot that he didn't always act as if he were enlightened, the teacher laughed and told him that was good because otherwise Jack would still imagine that he could find the Buddha outside of himself.

—Jack Kornfield

One repays a teacher badly if one remains only a pupil. Now I bid you lose me and find yourselves; and only when you have denied me will I return to you.

—Nietzsche's Zarathustra

4

Longing for the Divine Human: The Search for Spiritual Communion

When we find a spiritual teacher or guide who evokes our soul's longing, the *imago dei* leaps out of our inner world onto an ideal human being. Like mythic Hindu *gopis* worshiping Krishna or contemporary Siddha Yoga devotees adoring Gurumayi; like Hasidic students studying with their revered Rebbe or Sufi dervishes whirling around their *sheikh*, we are filled with exalted feelings of devotion in the presence of our ideal. The fires of our longing burn brighter when the revered one is near.

The teacher—priest, guru, *tzaddik, roshi, lama, sheikh*—has realized in human form the ideal Other living within the student, the *imago* of the complete or self-realized human being. They meet as two individuals with all of their gifts and limitations, wisdom and ignorance. But in the inner world the teacher carries the student's own highest authority, the parent who won't fail him, the god-like human whose attributes she strives to emulate. For the student to recognize the teacher as such, there must be some match between the inner image and the outer person, some subtle symmetry that enables the inward "yes."

A friend, Jennifer, wrote of such a life-altering meeting with an Indian meditation master:

> If there are words in the English language that precisely describe my feelings for Swami, I don't know them. They resembled the way I felt when I saw Elvis as a twelve-year-old on the Ed Sullivan show, as he shook and twisted and I screamed at cried at the television set. They also resembled an ancient, virgin love for my father that had long since disappeared with alcohol, mistakes, and just plain time. They resembled the way I felt when I was five and heard a Christmas carol for the first time—"Away in a manger no crib for a

bed, the little lord Jesus lay down his sweet head." I cried for several days, and no one had been able to explain the feeling to me, not for 42 years.

The closest thing to an explanation seems to be one of those ecstatic experiences that you hear of nuns having, who were considered either saintly or insane. But why would the sensible daughter of two atheists spontaneously combust like that? Where does this longing come from?

I have no answer to these questions. But Swami's presence made the feelings seem rooted in my own particular sanity. I had no shame when my heart raced as he entered the meditation hall; I felt alive with joy as I burst into spontaneous tears when I caught a glimpse of him close-up strolling through the dining hall. I would stand on the *darshan* line for an hour if need be, waiting to greet him. I'd bring an apple or a flower and wait. If he dismissed me, I had been false or self-effacing or needy or too sure of myself. If he welcomed me, I blushed and floated off in heaven, stumbling over the others sitting around me. Or I'd diminish my happiness, telling myself he must be having an expansive day and smiling at everyone like that. Or I thought he must not be so very wise if he smiled at me, black soul that I was.

Swami was beautiful, even at 72. He had brown skin with grey shadows. His voice had little bells in it as he sat cross-legged and told us about god dwelling inside of us. Sometimes, when he lectured, I would drift away, so full of this feeling I have no words for that I heard nothing. The conventional wisdom was that Swami generated so much spiritual energy that people could absorb his words in this half-asleep state. The waves of it were thick enough to drink and digest.

One evening I waited on the *darshan* line, weeping spontaneously, and decided to speak with him. I had seen people pour out their troubles, and I'd never done more than say hello or tell him of my gratitude. The time had come to take what was mine. I trembled so that I could hardly hang onto myself. The music from the visiting sitar player filled the hall. At last, I stepped forward and knelt before Baba. The words tumbled out. The tears, too. He looked right at me, his eyes just drinking me in, it seemed.

"My husband doesn't understand about you, Swami. I love you more than I love him."

I don't know what I thought he would do, maybe tell me that I should leave such a man, or tell me to bring my husband to him, or tell me it was a stupid complaint. Instead, he began to giggle, his little mouth crinkling up. He ruffled my hair and said, in a conspiratorial way, "Don't tell him about us. Just keep it a secret."

I nodded and bowed like I was supposed to. "Your feelings for me cannot hurt anyone. You must never be ashamed, never feel guilty. Now don't cry, you're too serious," he said. I looked up and he was peering at the person behind me. Our meeting was over.

I glided through the next few months. I kept the mantra alive in me at all times, internally bowing to god, as I stood in the kitchen peeling tomatoes, as my husband lectured me on the evils of his lead guitar player, as my tiny son spoke about his trials in nursery school. I loved going to bed because I could lie in the dark and think about Swami and god and light and warmth in a garden of unearthly pleasures—and the garden was all mine.

Once activated, this teacher-student archetype holds a promise and a duty, an inspiration and a burden. It summons us to the greater life; it calls for the death of all that stands in the way. It offers ultimate hope, even salvation; it requires an everlasting commitment to consciousness, kindness, and a higher ethical standard. And in most cases, at some point, it demands a meeting with the shadow.

Priest or teacher as parent: the psychology of spirituality

Whoever does not accept the kingdom of god like a child will never enter it.

—Jesus Christ

What would lead us to endow another human being with so much power and authority that we feel a blind faith in him or her? Our tender yearnings for the divine activate vulnerable feelings of childlike devotion. One client, a married woman, told me that she trusted and adored her rabbi, who seemed to her like the ideal man: handsome but not vain, smart but not patronizing, caring but not intrusive. When he told her that a sexual relationship with him would heal her childhood injuries, she didn't question him. Although both were married, she consented to an affair. A year later, devastated and ashamed, she called me for help. She loved the teachings and practice of Judaism, but felt rage at her rabbi and needed to reconcile her feelings and beliefs.

A student of kundalini yoga told me that upon meeting his Sikh teacher, he was mesmerized. He wanted the spiritual power of that man. So, he joined his community, practiced intensively, and eventually wore white robes and a turban, although this caused him great distress at his workplace. Several years later, when the teacher arranged his marriage to a stranger, this man wanted to prove his commitment to the teacher, so he agreed. Then, when the teacher sent the young son of that union off to India alone, he gave his permission again. A decade later, he felt confusion and regret about his decisions, but was too anxious to leave the teacher and face life without his community. He came to see me to do spiritual shadow-work.

As Freud pointed out, each of us carries unmet childhood needs into adulthood, such as an unconscious longing to merge with a powerful figure for protection against frightening feelings of powerlessness. Therefore, each of us is susceptible to the vagaries of human authorities, who appear to be benign and legitimate. Because Freudians believe only in our personal history and only in individual ego, for them our longing for an almighty Other can refer only to a parent. Therefore, a projection onto a teacher or priest involves a parent *imago*, and religion is a replay of childhood.

Although I don't see this as the complete explanation, I do see it as a partial truth. From this perspective, we can understand how a 50-year-old woman, an independent entrepreneur, suddenly acts childlike in relation to a spiritual teacher, unconsciously activating the parent/child archetype while trying to satisfy her early unmet needs. If she fuses internally with her teacher in order to derive strength from a parent *imago*, she is reliving the symbiotic level of relationship. If she projects god-like qualities onto him, she is returning to the magic level, imagining that she is protected by thinking and behaving like god himself. If her sense of self is more differentiated, she may return to the mythic level and call on her teacher to intervene in her life or in the world through prayer, meditation, or devotional rituals.

This regression in service of the ego enables the woman to locate an image of god in the Other, providing a connection to something greater than her individuality, even to something eternal. If the relationship is benevolent, it may help her to repair certain wounds, solidify her own ego, and fill unmet needs from these ages of childhood. For instance, in loving service to her teacher, she may come to feel worthy, even special. In the best-case scenario, if the teacher holds the projection temporarily but eventually guides her back to her own higher wisdom, the regression will have served its purpose.

But if the projection remains unconscious indefinitely, and the teacher perpetuates it, she may come to worship a person as god. And she may become trapped in a position of submission. Her feelings of being special and being somebody may merely mask deeper feelings of being empty and being nobody. She may work to build the teacher's church instead of building her own. In order to avoid excommunication and increase her sense of belonging, she may conform to totalitarian group dynamics. And, in an effort to avoid abandonment and maintain the precious relationship, she may comply with abusive, humiliating requests.

This woman's longing to be seen and to feel special may be enhanced by the possession of a secret, which ties her to the teacher and to the group. Initiated into a sacred mystery, she may vow to keep a spiritual practice confidential. Or she may become aware of the teacher's shadow, which binds her to him. Like the secret of sexual abuse in families that are bound together in a conspiracy of silence, the secret of spiritual abuse in religious communities acts like glue, reinforcing submission and compliance.

Heinz Kohut's self-psychology has extended our understanding of the emotional needs underlying our holy longing. According to Kohut, our individuality is shaped only in relation to others; it is embedded in their responses and cannot be understood apart from this human context. Therefore, Kohut does not use the dualistic language of self and other. He does not see one individual projecting her subjectivity onto another, such as a student/child unconsciously attributing power to a teacher/parent. Instead, Kohut and his followers use the term *selfobject,* which includes the subjectivity of both people and implies their inherent connection. Each is a *selfobject* to the other.

For Kohut, the relationship of a believer to god—in which the figure of a perfect and omnipotent deity with whom the imperfect and powerless believer wants to merge—corresponds to the early *selfobject* of baby and idealized parent *imago.* The believer longs to regain her original state of (pre-personal) union and attempts to do so by turning away from imperfection and constructing a religious relationship that protects her vulnerable ego.

With this emerging relationship, the aspirant longs for mirroring. If she becomes a valuable follower of a priest or teacher, she experiences an omniscient, omnipresent god as completely attuned to her every need. She does not, of course, see the other person in actuality, with all of his flaws and shortcomings, but uses him to foster her own sense of self-esteem and specialness.

Similarly, the teacher enjoys the admiration and devotion of the student. In this kind of relationship, each may come to overvalue or undervalue the other, depending on their needs. This may help to explain why some teachers exact such exclusive devotion from their followers.

In addition, the aspirant longs for an encounter with an ideal and therefore attributes qualities of perfection to the teacher. Ideal-hungry people, Kohut wrote, are always in search of others whom they can revere for their prestige, power, beauty, intelligence, or moral stature. Then, through a process of fusion, the student unconsciously identifies with the teacher's attainments and feels soothed.

These satisfying experiences serve to intensify the believer's commitment to the religious relationship and motivate him to ensure an ongoing connection. He may rely on dogma and a literal interpretation of text to reinforce the relationship, as we can observe in fundamentalists of any tradition. But, paradoxically, this closed system prevents him from further developing his own separate sense of self.

If the student's self-worth develops via mirroring and her capacity for self-soothing develops via idealizing the teacher, then the relationship will have served healthy aims. Even if the connection to the idealized teacher is broken through a disappointment, the student may be able to reclaim projections and perceive the teacher more accurately, more humanly.

This was Jennifer's experience, as the story above unfolded:

> When Swami went back to India with his lucky entourage, he left behind a small group of followers who were supposed to keep his love alive for me. But it wasn't like that. When I thought of him, I cried and cried. Eventually, I lost touch with the intensity of the feeling and just drifted away from it, as I had after my father left.
>
> Meanwhile, my husband's unhappiness grew like a fast-spreading tumor. It took all of my guts to get out of that house, but I did it in a week. I went from room to room in the new house and filled them with pictures of Swami as I chanted the mantra. I even put a picture in my son's room. But I didn't feel like Swami knew how much pain I suffered. I wasn't sure he was really still there at all.
>
> One day my girlfriend Jill called. She and her husband had met Swami when I brought them to him. Her husband had fallen like a ton of bricks, and she had resisted. She felt excluded and suspicious since her husband had begun chanting and eating tofu and reading books on Eastern religion. She worshipped Henry James and Proust and filled herself up with them at night as I had with Swami.
>
> "I'm so fed up with David," she announced. "Now he's all upset about the Swami scandal. It's even more annoying than Swami himself."
>
> "What scandal?" I asked after a small hesitation.

"You don't know. Oh, Jenny, you shouldn't hear this from me."

"What scandal, Jill?" Adrenaline rushed through my body.

"Oh, I don't know, it's probably a rumor. But people said that several of Swami's followers claim that he sexually molested their daughters. He said he wanted to check to see if they were virgins. David said there are always scandals around holy men, especially when they're about to die. They have to test their followers."

"About to die?" I whispered.

"He's sick, Jenny, a heart condition. This is the last year before he leaves his body." She used that phrase with a certain contempt.

"I didn't know ..." My words faded away. I felt dizzy.

In some way, this information was simply unbearable. This was no time to lose my Swami. These scandals meant nothing. He would be my guru dead or alive. So, I created a mask, the mask of the devotee, and I became a more articulate devotee than I had been before. I had more trappings in my house. I set up an altar and burned incense. I read Swami's books, even though they bored me. I no longer felt the rapture and protection of his love as I drifted off to sleep. But I no longer remembered it, so it didn't matter.

Six months later, David called. "I thought I should let you know before you heard it from Jill," he said. "Swami died. Heart attack."

"Okay, thanks." I hung up. Something unstoppable came over me. A thunderstorm. I wailed, I raged. The world had looked so sweet for that one year. Now it seemed like a moment. I was sure I would understand one day what happened with those girls. But now he was gone, vanished. He had left me, stolen my heart and disappeared. There was no magic. I'd been a sucker.

I didn't cry after that day. I never allowed myself to tell anyone how I really felt. I never betrayed the memory of Swami out loud. I hid my disillusionment and loss, and the slender thread of faith snapped. It had been so delicate, that was part of its beauty. It had been so silvery and had given me my life back. Now it wasn't just out of reach; it was gone.

In retrospect, Jennifer told me that she learned to coexist with different truths about her teacher. "He radiated an inner beauty that I'd never seen before. And it was intoxicating, almost sexual, like the rush of a drug. So, I couldn't believe those rumors. They didn't mesh with my experience. I didn't want him to be *that*—cruel and deceptive.

"On the other hand, I became cynical and didn't want to admit it. But it was revealed in my actions, not my words. I didn't meditate anymore. I didn't do the practices, even though I thought I believed in them. The chanting tapes had helped to calm and center me. But they also stopped my thoughts. These two realities sat side by side."

During that time, another devotee, a friend of Jennifer's, wrote a novel and received an offer to publish it from an excellent New York house. When the friend informed her teacher about it, he told her not to make the agreement. The ashram would publish it. The devotee agreed.

Jennifer was outraged. "How could you consent to this?" she asked.

"I've moved to a place where I don't make my own decisions. And I like it that way," the friend stated.

Jennifer looked into the mirror of her friend's behavior, and the reflection startled her. She recalled a hymn from a childhood church: "I'll go where you want me to go, Dear Lord, O'er mountain or plain or sea. I'll say what you want me to say, Dear Lord, I'll be what you want me to be." Understandably, that kind of obedience and dependency seemed to her to be regressive and dysfunctional. For Jennifer, the withdrawal of the projection opened the doorway to the Self.

But, for other people, identification with the projection may be a valid spiritual path, assuming it is not exploitative. Within the context of the Catholic tradition or a guru lineage, for example, we may re-experience unmet dependency needs in a positive way through a relationship with Christ via a priest or through devotion to a spiritual teacher. Just as an intimate partnership can serve as a container in which we develop, a spiritual partnership also can contain and stimulate our growth, helping us to reclaim lost parts of the self and move toward higher levels of development.

However, there is great danger here: a believer may lose her autonomy, her voice, and her will if she surrenders them to the wrong person. She may risk not living her own life.

Today Jennifer is grateful for the love that opened her heart. But she also lives with a feeling of loss. When I asked her where her holy longing goes now, she replied, "I visit a Catholic church. I was raised as an atheist, but I used to cry for the baby Jesus. Now the organ, the incense, the Mass give me joy. I won't convert, but I'm most happy in a church."

In some cases of the teacher, priest, or rabbi failing to carry the *imago* indefinitely, either through revealing a human limitation or acting out a shadow, a wrenching separation ensues. The student may need to turn the teacher into an adversary (or adversarial *selfobject*) in order to push against him and separate from him, thereby confirming her own autonomy, much like an adolescent who finds identity by pushing against a parent.

However, the aspirant may lose the soothing relationship without internalizing his own self-worth or sense of authority. Left on his own, he may come to believe in the omnipotence of his own mind and rigidly adhere to his own dogmatic, concrete thinking in an effort to replace the presence of the idealized Other. Rather than addressing his own thwarted longings, the believer masks the trauma of disappointment by retrenching in a belief system.

One such man, who felt abandoned by his priest, sought out like-minded believers in a militant cult to reinforce his own conclusions and protect his fragile sense of identity. When he entered therapy, he insisted that I agree completely with his worldview, or he could not trust me.

A woman client came to see me after a series of disappointing relationships with Buddhist meditation teachers. Each separation from a teacher was a heartbreaking rite of passage, in which her sense of self fragmented as each projection snapped. Therefore, she left with angry negative feelings and continued to hope that the next great figure would not disappoint her but would become the all-loving father she never had and, even more, the all-wise god-figure.

She could not break this ideal-seeking pattern until she internalized her own spiritual ideal. Many years later, she was able to approach spiritual mentors again and to learn from them because she no longer set them on pedestals from which, inevitably, they would fall.

Eventually, I, too, came to see how my first meditation teacher, more than thirty years ago, was a substitute father or, more accurately, a shadow father: the stable quality of his presence was reassuring and calming. The compassionate quality of his message lifted me up out of myself, beyond narcissistic concerns. His promise that we would attain enlightenment through practice eased my terrors of aging and death.

Finally, his values overturned those I had internalized from my own father. My relation to him was an aid on my way to independence, that is, to choosing values that separated me from my tightly knit family. But eventually, I had to develop those values for myself that were dictated neither by my spiritual father nor by my biological father.

Of course, individual psychology is formed in a cultural milieu. Our susceptibility to authoritarian personalities begins at home and is fostered by our social institutions as well. Many parents override natural feelings of vulnerability, dependency, and sadness in their children, banishing these emotions into the unconscious shadow. They teach their children that these emotions are not acceptable because *they* were taught to disown them through their parents' contempt or their teachers' punishment or their clergy's shaming words. But these feelings remain in the darkness over the years, so that no matter how independent an adult appears, an inner child's longing for a powerful, protective parent remains.

Or adults may punish a child for temper tantrums, teaching him that his anger, which may even be justified, is not acceptable. Eventually, the anger, buried in the darkness, no longer surfaces. And when the young man is abused by his father/priest, he cannot feel his rage; he can only continue to protect his abuser and blame himself.

Many schools and institutionalized religions add to the mix because authoritarianism is woven into the context and content of their teachings. In fact, their ideologies, as well as their means of transmitting those ideologies, often lead us to mistrust ourselves by rewarding obedience to external authority, punishing independent thinking, and seeding guilt and shame. For example, nuns repeatedly told a grade-school boy that he was "too big for his britches." Now he cannot feel his own successes forty years later. Rather than take any credit for his business achievements, he claims that he is merely god's instrument.

A Catholic client developed an irrational fear of doctors who carried for her the voice of a god-like authority—the ability to pronounce a blessing or a curse. Because both her father and priest taught her that she was born in sin and deserved to be punished, she saw illness as her just reward. And she gave the power over it, and so over her body, to the male doctors whom she feared.

If a child associates feeling loved with feeling shamed, flawed, and worthless, then these feelings will seem familiar when they arise in religious discipleships. Several long-term meditators whom I know feel ashamed before their guru because they have not attained a certain level of practice after many years. Each of them had a father who demanded a high level of performance from them; now they seek spiritual perfection in order to gain approval from their spiritual father.

Demaris Wehr has pointed out that authority does not only mean the right to enforce obedient conduct in others. It also refers to the author of an idea or expert in a field. Perhaps, she said, by reclaiming both our authority and our vulnerability, we can learn to be authors of our own lives.

Certainly, if we can carry our vulnerable shadows more consciously, they will inoculate us against the dangers of our own power shadows. They will remind us of our humanity and protect us from superior self-righteousness. On the other hand, when we relinquish our authority to another and banish our vulnerability to the shadow, we are at risk of falling into self-righteous aggression, which we witness everywhere today.

Just as it's not sufficient to say that the parent is the final and only source of the god image, it's also not sufficient to say that the parent is the only source of the teacher *imago*. Mythologist Mircea Eliade pointed out that it's our need to realize archetypes, our longing for transcendent forms that reveals something about our place in the cosmos.

Priest or teacher as god: the archetypes of spirituality

The decisive question for [a human being] is: Is he related to something infinite or not?

—C.G. Jung

While Freud's exploration of the parent *imago* and the personal transference in therapy was groundbreaking, Jung took the next step: archetypal transference. The German root of the term "transference" means to carry something over from one place to another. In its psychological use, emotions that are overwhelming to one person are attributed to another person, forming a tie between the two. As a special case of projection, transference is the emotional link between a patient and a therapist in which the patient clings to the promise of change and renewal via the therapist. I suggest that the same process takes place between a believer and a spiritual guide.

Archetypal transference has hidden within it not only the image of a parent; it carries the image of an archetype or divine *imago*, such as the Self, which brings meaning and purpose to life. When a living teacher becomes the object of our unconscious ideal through projection of the Self, a link is made: the student-lover longs for union with the teacher-beloved, who is typically unavailable in a personal way, thus creating an agonizing sense of separation, which fuels the fires of longing. This inherent separation, (*viraha* in Sanskrit), is the basis for certain devotional practices, such as *bhakti* yoga, which can bring on ecstatic and erotic states of yearning.

In a classical spiritual apprenticeship, the student is encouraged to meditate on the teacher as the image of god, deliberately merge with him or her, and even give over the sense of individual authority and control. This process relieves the terrible anxiety that accompanies our existential uncertainty: suddenly, we are in the presence of someone who knows the truth. If we behave properly, if we maintain our faith, we, too, will know the truth.

But this dynamic leads to a questionable assumption: a human being can have divine authority. If the teacher knows the truth, he must be morally superior, even infallible. If so, he must be immune to the corruptions of the shadow, immune to the abuse of power, and immune to self-interest. If we follow this line of reasoning to its end, the teacher also must be immune to making mistakes. So, any behavior that seems questionable to believers cannot be questioned: given the teacher's level of consciousness, it *must* stem from pure motives and right action.

The same principle holds in any tradition: if the priest is a representative of the Pope, and the Pope is the elect of Christ, then he must know more and we must follow his edicts without question. If the head Hasidic rabbi, known as the Lubavitcher rebbe, is seen by his disciples as the Messiah, then whatever he says must be the truth and must be obeyed completely.

But there are inherent dangers for the ardent believer who projects the divine Self onto a living human being:

- the risk of giving our own spiritual radiance to another and thereby losing contact with our own divinity. When we attribute the superior light of the Self to another, we fail to know our own essence within. I have found in my work with many clients that it is not only our darkness that we disown; it is our spiritual light, our natural radiance, which we hide. And when we give it away to a "higher" teacher, we see it only outside ourselves.

- the risk of giving our powers of discrimination and independent thinking to another and thereby losing trust in our own minds. When we attribute greater wisdom to another, we gradually fail to believe our own instincts and intuition. If we join a church group or spiritual community even though something doesn't feel quite right; if we commit to a doctrine even though we have grave doubts; if we use practices or dogma to ward off uncertainty, we are slowly being trained to obey external authority, rather than our own minds. Eventually, we will come to think that doubt is a sin, disbelieving the teacher is disbelieving god.

- the risk of giving our emotional authority to another and thereby losing trust in our own authentic feelings. When we believe that another person knows what's best for our emotional well-being, we begin to turn away from our own fear, anger, shame, and depression, each of which is a cue about the spiritual relationship and its environment. Eventually, we will have ceded control of our inner landscape to another, and our vital emotional truths will be silenced.

- Finally, our holy longing makes us susceptible to spiritual authority and authoritarianism, to authentic spiritual power and to power shadow. We risk giving our loving obedience to a teacher who may abuse us, recreating a pattern of wounding, instead of healing. When the arrow of projection carries spirit and lands on a human being, he potentially controls her soul.

Jung told the story of a patient whose persistent transference to him revealed collective religious qualities that appeared to be larger and deeper than her personal unconscious material. That is, he could not attribute her projections merely to her father and her family history. The woman's fantasies about Jung grew more and more fantastic as they explored them together. As she endowed him with superhuman traits, she experienced herself with daughter-like dependence.

She dreamed, for example, that she was a tiny child in the arms of her father, who was a giant. The giant stood in a wheat field. As the wind swept over the field, the giant swayed back and forth, rocking the child.

In response to this dream, Jung wondered whether the patient's unconscious was "trying to create a god out of the person of the doctor." It seemed to him that she was unconsciously trying to free a vision of god from the veils of the person. If this were the case, her unconscious only appeared to be reaching out toward Jung, the man. In a deeper sense, it was really reaching out toward a god. This led him to wonder whether the soul's longing for a god could be even stronger than its love for a person.

Although Jung could not be the god-man of the patient's fantasies, the *imago dei* that was fueling the transference could be. When the patient consciously realized the religious content of her transference onto Jung, she became freed of her dependence on him as a man. The transference to her analyst was resolved, so to speak, because her projections linked back to their archetypal sources. He was no longer the god whom she loved—but the carrier of the god image by means of which she loved.

Like all symbols, the archetypal mother also represents the Self or god image. When Jung named a specific *imago* as an object of longing, he was acknowledging that the source of longing is not found in a reductive understanding of personal history alone; it is the Self longing for itself.

Eastern traditions have taught this message in a different language for millennia. In the *Bhagavad Gita*, the warrior Arjuna stands paralyzed on the battlefield facing members of his own family. He knows his duty—to fight—but his heart is in moral conflict. He prays for the assistance of something greater than himself. At that moment of spiritual crisis, the divine *avatar*, or incarnation of god, appears as Krishna.

Like the Self in relation to the ego (Arjuna), Krishna stands behind the warrior as a hidden transpersonal center. He does not tell him what to do or how to do it; he simply articulates one teaching: how the divine in Arjuna can live in direct relation to the divine Krishna. As one translator summed it up, "Established in yoga (or union with the divine), perform action."

Like Arjuna acting in service to Krishna, the ego can be relativized and act in service to the Self. It no longer acts for its own outcomes, with attachment to its own goals, but acts with the freedom of non-attachment, offering the fruits of its actions to the divine. Some current *advaita* teachers speak about this as the absence of the doer, the one who lays claim to action and will.

Certain gurus describe this as their level of development. Jung referred to them as *mana*-personalities—the hero, chief, magician, medicine-man, saint, friend of god. He referred to the female counterpart as a sublime matriarchal figure, the great mother who understands and forgives everything, lives only for others, and never seeks her own interests. Jung wrote that the *mana*-personality evolves into a hero or godlike being, whose earthly expression is the priest. Today we know that a rabbi, *sheikh*, *lama*, or spiritual director can become a *mana*-personality as well.

When this charismatic personality is activated in the teacher, a feeling of creaturely dependence is activated in the student, as it was in Jung's patient. She can place her responsibilities at his feet. She can stop thinking for herself or acting from her own agency. And, through turning him into a god, she can become a knower of reality by association with him.

These living masters can appear via many archetypal images. For example, if we long for certainty, which brings an end to the anxiety of living with the unknown, we may be drawn to the wise old man or woman—the *senex*. This figure offers the order of morality and the certainty of knowledge. Like the Dalai Lama as seen by some followers, he may carry the wisdom of authority like a compassionate mentor. Or, like the Pope as seen by some critics, he may appear distant and rigid, like an old king making decrees.

As James Hillman pointed out in *Puer Papers*, the *senex* is the opposite of the *puer aeternus* or eternal youth. The nature of our *senex* qualities reflects the degree of our own connection with the *puer* archetype, who keeps us open to fresh possibilities and to the vital imagination. If the wise old man or woman loses contact with his own inner *puer* qualities, he may yearn for someone to carry them on the outside. This dynamic may help to explain why some teachers, who appear so self-sufficient, yearn for disciples to follow them, and even to complete them.

While the *senex's* masculinity may be one-sided, the *puer's* femininity may compensate. While the *senex* maintains rules and boundaries, the *puer* is fiery, inquisitive, and non-committal.

At a mythological level, the *puer aeternus* is the archetype of spirit. Like Icarus, he flies high over the world, free and unattached, unable to live an embodied life. This divine figure can keep us connected to ideals and a genuine spirituality. But, possessed by it, a man or woman may suffer from an inability to mature, conform, or commit to life in this world. The *puer* or *puella* may wander eternally, always longing for something better, unable to settle into a routine of any kind. He may appear innocent and childish, caught in fantasies of spiritual perfection. He may be unable to accept the limits of mortal life. In Jung's terms, he is trapped in spirit and unable to incarnate instinct.

In *The Wounded Woman*, Linda Leonard described female carriers of this archetype as wounded daughters trying to free themselves from a father complex. The *puella* woman may identify with her father and remain undeveloped or become an addict, displacing her dependency onto a substance. Or she may rebel and lose her own connection to spirit, becoming rigid and father-like herself. Or she may marry a *senex* and project the authority that she lacks within onto him.

I would add that a *puella* woman may become devoted to a *senex* teacher and remain in a suspended childlike state as the King's daughter. In this condition, her own spiritual capacity remains projected outside of her, and she is always the special child, the princess, but not a divine person in her own right.

If we long for salvation, we may be drawn to the teacher who appears as savior, prophet, or messiah. The believer who feels sinful or flawed yearns for redemption from the one who has purified his sins or cleansed his karma. These saviors, such as Christ and Mohammed, tend to bring a message that is exclusive to their believers and focused on the next world, after the rapture, after the jihad.

If we long for unconditional love, we may be drawn to the teacher who appears as divine mother. The Indian female teachers Amachi and Mother Meera embrace their spiritual children in silent acceptance, and wounded hearts are healed.

If we long for faith, we may be drawn to the teacher who appears as shaman or magician because he can demonstrate special powers (or *siddhis*). The Indian teacher Sai Baba's reportedly breathtaking feats of materialization give believers the hope of escaping human limitations.

If we long to break free of the bounds of rationality and conventionality, even the constraints of morality, we may be drawn to the teacher who appears as trickster. He or she stands outside of the social order and provokes our unasked questions about the arbitrariness of sacred customs and values. Like G.I. Gurdjieff, Bhagwan Shri Rajneesh (Osho), Chogyam Trungpa Rinpoche, and Da Free John, the trickster uses shock, clowning, physical force, nudity, alcohol, and drugs to awaken followers from the trance of consensual thinking. Rather than bringing order, he brings disorder; rather than harmony, disharmony. In this way, he shows the limits of our rational minds and points the way toward non-dual awareness, in which all opposites are reconciled.

After studying Indian and Chinese scripture and philosophy, Jung took a stand against the Eastern teacher/disciple model. He proposed instead that his form of analysis could bring about a conscious reunion of the ego with the Self. By reclaiming the unconscious contents that we attribute to the charismatic personality, he said, we come back to ourselves, to our own treasury, to that part of us that is so strange, yet so near—the Self.

I strongly agree with Jung that no god should be constructed out of the archetype of the *mana*-personality. In other words, he or she should be seen as having human greatness and human limitations. However, I also understand discipleship as a stage in human development that can become an appropriate step in maturation. That is, the projection of the Self can be a precursor to the awakening of the Self within—if psychological work is a part of the spiritual relationship.

In fact, Jung himself became a *mana*-personality in his time and remains so today for some people who call themselves "Jungian." For many, he serves well as teacher, mentor, and ancestor. But other Jungians, despite espousing individuality as the peak of human development, appear to require conformity in therapeutic principles and practice. Some have lost Jung's spirit of exploration and experimentation and insist, instead, that students subordinate their own soul's journey to one that looks like his. A few, sadly, have turned to *imitatio* Jung as their response to uncertainty. In the worst cases, they use Jung's shadow behaviors to justify their own destructive acting out.

Jungian analyst James Yandell put it poignantly when he asked: in order to be a Jungian, do I have to subordinate my individuality to communal standards? But, if I do that, then I am no longer, by definition, a Jungian.

Fortunately, there are many analysts today who feel tremendous respect, even awe for Jung's genius, but also see his shadow sides. They can admit the shortcomings in his work, attempt to build bridges with other psychologies, and remain open to dialogue.

I appreciate Yandell's paradoxical conclusion to his own relationship with Jung's *mana*-personality, which he described in a pamphlet entitled "Imitatio Jung": "The only way I can emulate Jung in the deepest sense is by living out my own identity and realizing my own potential as fully as Jung lived out his. But if I were a Jungian in this sense, it's unlikely that I would submit myself to a training program, affiliate with a society of analysts, or identify with a movement. And without these things, I would not be a Jungian."

During the years of founding his first institute, Jung was prescient about this issue when he said, "Thank God I'm Jung—and not a Jungian!"

Clearly, when we concretize and literalize the *imago dei* as a fallible human being, this relationship dynamic can evoke many dangers. But, on the other hand, to discard discipleship simply and entirely is to lose the gifts of a timeless pattern of relationship. Perhaps it would be best to say, with Ken Wilber, that ideally we should set out on a spiritual quest having done our psychological homework. That is, we should have attained to the rational level of development, in which the ego is consolidated. Then the *imago* has a place within which to reside. But this ideal sequence is rare among the enlightened people I know, as I will discuss later.

Or, we might follow Jung's suggestion to turn toward our own souls, which offer an inner initiation via our dreams and creativity. In this way Jung encountered the internal figure of Philemon, a wise old man with horns and wings, who acted for him much like a guide or *imago dei*. The Hindu saint Ramakrishna also met an inner wise man, a yogi or *sannyasi*, who initiated him from within.

In Jung's language, our holy longing fuels the journey from preconscious unity toward conscious reconciliation with the Self. He saw this process, which he called individuation, as the purpose of human life. He must have felt the holy longing intensely when he wrote, "The individual who is not anchored in god can offer no resistance on his own resources to the physical and moral blandishments of the world. For this he needs the evidence of inner, transcendent experience, which alone can protect him from the otherwise inevitable submersion in the mass."

Jung intuitively followed his own longing through dusky cellars, blue seas, and black nights, as he mapped the archetypal realm. Rather than reject holy longing, as Freud did, or romanticize it, as those possessed by spirit do, he lived his life in direct relationship to it without human intermediaries.

In the end, Jung knew the danger of reducing the ineffable to words. He pointed out that psychology touches on the phenomenology of spirit but not on the essential nature of it. If its essence could be explained, it would become merely a subdivision of psychology. And its mystery would be lost.

For those of us who have experienced the enormity of the meeting with the divine in human form, the concepts of personal and archetypal projection do not suffice somehow. Although we need to beware of the risks, we also need to dwell more deeply in the mystery.

Priest or teacher as divine human: the teacher/student relationship

There is no deity superior to the guru, no gain better than the guru's grace, no state higher than meditation on the guru.

—Swami Muktananda

From a purely scientific or psychological point of view, spiritual teachers are irrelevant: they are artifacts of our projections. But there are human beings among us who have attained the psychic, subtle, causal, and non-dual levels of development, however rare. And from a spiritual point of view, these saints and sages are more evolved along the path of consciousness, closer to the end point of union with the divine.

Along with their other tasks as teachers—to model a way of life, instruct in spiritual teachings, transmit a level of consciousness, and awaken our holy longing—they knowingly carry the Self or *imago dei* for others. As an embodiment of the attributes of god, a spiritual teacher represents the fulfillment of human longing.

In this Sufi story, *sheikh* Jafar al-Sadiq is aware of his task. A man insulted him, so Jafar went to the man's house. "When you said those things, I made no reply. If the qualities you attribute to me are really in me, I give you my word that I shall repent of them. But if the qualities you ascribed to me are not in me, I pray to God that he pardon you. I forgive you what you said and don't hold it against you." The man fell at the *sheikh*'s feet and repented.

In many contemplative traditions, this relationship and its projection are accepted and encouraged as an essential part of the spiritual journey. In the various sects of Tibetan Buddhism, the *lamas*' lineages can be traced back for many generations. Among Hasidic Jews, the head rabbi has near-divine authority. Among Sufis, the *pir* or *sheikh* demands respect and obedience due to his station or level of consciousness. And among certain Hindu sects, the dependency that results from this relationship is even encouraged: the master acquires power of attorney from his disciples so that their financial dependency triggers emotional dependency, which can potentially be transformed into spiritual dependency.

So, from a Western point of view, the disciple projects the Self, and the teacher receives it. But from an Eastern point of view, the reverse occurs: the teacher radiates energy, or *darshan*, and the devotee internalizes (or introjects) it like food. That is, from a higher level of consciousness, the master broadcasts god, and the student absorbs the vibrations.

As a result, the student feels expansive, even blissful. And she may come to rely on this state, even depend on it. Soon, the teacher appears to be the gatekeeper to her experience of peace of mind, open-heartedness, meaning, and purpose—the only gatekeeper.

As the student projects the *imago dei*, and the teacher absorbs it; as the teacher gives *darshan* and the student absorbs it, the pattern is set. Each becomes responsible in some subtle way for the inner reality of the Other. Each begins to perceive the Other through the blinders of their level of consciousness and its *imago*.

The teacher may come to believe that she can surrender her individuality in order to sustain the projection of the Self for her devotees. Conversely, the student may attempt to surrender his individuality prematurely to become the ideal follower. In the end, both try to do an end run around emotional issues to fulfill their roles. As a consequence, development occurs along certain lines (religious or spiritual), and not along others, (emotional, cognitive, or moral). And shadows are more likely to erupt.

Slowly, insidiously, teacher and student may come to hold each other in position via a kind of field that emerges between them. And both have a lot to lose if the field is pierced.

Jeffrey Masson, who has written widely about Freud, also wrote a less well-known book, *My Father's Guru*, in which he described this reciprocal process between his father and Paul Brunton, a teacher of mysticism who lived with the Masson family. "My father believed he was being singled out. He felt elevated and special in the presence of this special and elevated man. Only if P.B. (Brunton) was an adept with occult powers could my father maintain his special status, so it was important that he have these qualities. P.B. needed my father as much as my father needed him. He depended on the constant reassurance that a fawning acolyte could give. Certainly, my father wanted something no person could ever give him, and P.B. claimed to be able to give my father what no person can ever give another. One wanted, the other offered, transcendence of this world."

The inner marriage: A story of holy longing in the Christian saint Catherine of Siena

In 1347, in Siena, Italy, in a tall brick house with a tile roof, Catherine Benincasa and her twin sister were born. Their mother, who already had twenty-two babies, sent the sicker infant to a wet nurse and took Catherine to her own breast. The sister died soon after, and Catherine's Catholic mother reminded her daily that she had a special obligation to be good—god chose her to survive.

At five, Catherine loved to visit the small stone church of St. Dominic just up the hill from her house. She gazed at colorful icons of the saints and inhaled incense like the breath of life. When she returned home, hand in hand with her mother, and climbed the stairs leading up to her room, she bowed her blond head, genuflected, and poured her heart into Hail Marys on each step.

At seven, Catherine wandered through the town square, enraptured by the pinks and oranges of sunset. As she stood at the city gates gazing up at the sky, all at once Jesus appeared in the heavens, robed in white, and smiling at her. Behind him, a circle of saints in white awaited. A shaft of light fell on the small girl, who collapsed in the dirt.

From that day, the fire that Christians call the passion for Christ was lit in her. Yearning to be near him, she hid in a stone grotto to recite fervent prayers, vowing her virginity to Mary. She tied a rope into knots and flailed her tiny body in imitation of Christ's suffering until blue welts rose beneath the skin.

At 15, Catherine's mother and sister prepared her for marriage. But when this older sister died in 1362, Catherine blamed herself for the tragedy, for surviving the death of another cherished sister. She believed that her flirtation with worldliness during the preparation for marriage caused the death. As a result, she vowed that she would have no bridegroom but Christ. Her longing for Him and Him alone intensified.

Catherine struck a child's bargain with god: in exchange for her sacrifices, she would win salvation for her entire family. Her life of penance would give her power over the sins of her parents. On the contrary, if she yielded to desire, she would damn them forever. With defiance, she took a shears and cut her blond curls to the roots.

Trying to break her will, her parents took away her private room and assigned her the chores of washing, cooking, and sewing for the large household. In her mind she constructed a secret cell that no one could take from her, and her religiosity deepened. And in her imagination she turned her family into the holy family of Jesus, Mary, and the apostles and served them gladly.

At 16, she told her father decisively that she refused marriage. At first, he was distraught. But one day he entered her room silently while she was at prayer. A white dove, sign of the Holy Spirit, seemed to hover above her head. Startled at his daughter's unique spiritual gifts, he finally agreed to her vocation.

Catherine put on a rough wool robe with an iron chain against her hips. She gave up consuming meat and wine and consumed only bread, raw vegetables, and water. Her body wasted. She entered three years of silence, except for confession, and prayed incessantly to her bridegroom, Christ. She slept only thirty minutes every two days. And yet she continued to feel that she had not tamed her flesh and that she was an unworthy sinner.

Catherine cried inconsolably, begging her father to permit her to join the Sisters of Penance in the Dominican order. Eventually, she donned their long black mantle and white veil, while continuing to live among those she vowed to save.

Continuing rigorous fasts and endless prayers, she burst into tears on occasion. At other times, she leaned against a wall motionless, her face pale, seeing and hearing nothing, lost to this world. During one period, she heard persecuting voices and saw visions of naked people. She felt tormented and abandoned by Jesus. But, eventually, she was able to create distance from them and observe them, rather than feel overwhelmed by them. And, with that move, they lost their grasp.

First pious neighbors, then the Church began to take notice of her severe austerities and her single-minded devotion. When she was 27, they accused her of being fed by the devil because she had lived without eating for two years, which would continue for seven more. She begged god to help her to eat and tried to force herself. But by this time the loss of appetite was beyond her control. The pain on eating was so great that she forced stalks of fennel down her throat to induce vomiting. In the end, she could not even receive the sacrament of the host but felt content simply to be near it.

Despite these physical deprivations, Catherine devoted immense energy to church causes. She wrote letters and rallied supporters to urge the Pope to leave France and return to Rome. She worked ceaselessly giving charity to the poor and assisting victims of the plague, which ravaged Siena.

At the same time, Catherine's prayers focused on a single driving desire: to love others as Christ loved them. Her prayer was answered in the form of a vision: Jesus appeared and took out her heart, replacing it with his own.

After years of yearning for him, Catherine was betrothed to her bridegroom. She described an inner experience in which Jesus placed a bridal ring on her finger, fulfilling her years of devotion.

Catherine began to dictate four petitions to god while going in and out of ecstatic states. The result: the *Dialogue*, a complex exchange between Catherine and her beloved god.

At age 33, yearning to be fully united with god, she stopped drinking water in order to give her body back to Him. She died of starvation in 1380 and was canonized in 1461.

Clearly, Catherine's yearning for her bridegroom had a dark side, rooted in medieval Christian beliefs: In exchange for her parents' sins, which condemned them to eternal punishment, she dedicated herself to self-denial. Her "holy anorexia," as coined by Rudolph Bell in a book of that name, began with terrible guilt over surviving the deaths of her two sisters and the love of her worldly mother.

Experts on anorexia today point out that girls who feel forced to live for others and to meet their impossible high standards may go to extremes to try to control their own fates, such as conquering their bodily desires. Like Catherine, they may define themselves by striving for perfection through self-denial. And the pattern of conquest and reward that is set up through fasting and bingeing offers them a sense of mastery, a triumph over dependency, a saint-like victory. Like Christ, Catherine felt no desire, no pain, no hunger, and so became god-like in her own right.

Jungian analyst Marion Woodman has written of this link between love of spirit and rejection of bodily life in anorexic girls in *Addiction to Perfection*. She suggested that when we reject food, we reject matter, or life itself. We reject incarnation—or "down"—and seek to become pure spirit—or "up." But perfection belongs only to the gods, Woodman said. And the striving for spirit without flesh, light without darkness is a denial of human nature.

The stories of holy longing offer stark similarities and differences: Rumi, Ramakrishna, and Catherine had early childhood spiritual experiences, which opened a window onto other worlds. Today we would call them altered states of consciousness. But because of the passage of time and the particularity of their religious languages and structures, we don't really know their nature. However, we do know that with these experiences each of them awoke to a religious fervor and a basic dissatisfaction with the status quo.

For Catherine, that meant rejecting an arranged marriage and life in the footsteps of her mother. For Rumi, that meant rejecting a position as a scholar and life in the footsteps of his father. For Ramakrishna, that meant rejecting all convention. However, each of their sacrifices led to the gift of a spiritual marriage.

Differences appear in the objects of their longing. Rumi met a man who was for him an *insan al kamil*, a complete human being. Through intense communion with him, Rumi gave up his attachments to his earlier understandings, practices, and values, becoming a lover of music, poetry, and dance.

When separated from his beloved, first temporarily, then permanently, Rumi's yearning intensified nearly to the point of madness. Yet in the development of his poems we can see his evolution through the Sufi stations, or levels of consciousness, in a fairly orderly way.

Catherine's beloved Jesus was for her, too, a model of ideal human life. Through intense communion with him, she served others with the heart of Christ and strived to become his bride. In moments of ecstatic union with god, she wrote that her soul left her body and she attained her dream.

When we project the divine Self onto a priest or teacher, the opposites meet and marry: light and dark, divine and human, masculine and feminine, unlimited and limited, free and enslaved, purified and sinful. This process accounts for the sense of wholeness that arises from the union.

At certain levels of development, this student/teacher or lover/beloved relationship can be healing and urge evolution onward. In addition, people of a certain temperament, for example heart-centered devotional people, may require a human beloved as an object of their loving.

However, at a more developed stage, I believe this projection has to be left behind. An alchemical process, which could unfold within the soul, gets acted out on the interpersonal stage of life and can inhibit the turning within which is so needed. For example, if a saint, master, or rabbi stands in for the messiah, we are less likely to focus on our own messiah nature. If we depend on the unconditional love of a divine mother figure, we are less likely to cultivate that quality within our own hearts. If we place our faith on the outer performance of miracles, we are less likely to be called upon to develop a faith that is internally rooted. Finally, if an ideal Other is responsible for our sense of Self, then we may do just about anything to sustain it.

The result: rather than making a direct relationship to the divine in our own souls, we make the link through an intermediary. And a real, fallible human being is asked to stand in for the disowned qualities of the Self. He or she becomes the guardian of our *imago dei*. All too often, that person has the power to banish or excommunicate us from the community, denying us a felt sense of relationship to the divine.

If the student cannot see through the projection and turns the teacher into a god, coming to believe that this unattainable Other alone promises transcendence, then he is enslaved by the relationship; he is caught in idolatry. The image is mistaken for the god behind it.

On the other hand, if the student can link with the divine in his own soul—via contemplation of the *imago* in a teacher—then the aspirant is freed by the relationship. In this case, the *imago* acts as a window, not a wall.

And in this context, the teacher/student relationship becomes a container of Eros, the cosmic longing that leads us to higher and higher levels of transcendence—from a psychic glimpse of the Self to a subtle longing to lose the Self to a causal apperception of non-dual awareness, in which the image of the teacher disappears with all duality into union with the divine.

PART II

After the Fall:
A Guide for Disillusioned Believers

I cry to you, and you give me no answer;
I stand before you, but you take no notice.

—Job 30:19

A disciple asked a learned rabbi why god used to speak directly to the people but never does so today. The wise man replied, 'People cannot bend low enough now to hear what god says.'

—Jewish proverb

The whole world is pining for light and freedom. To respond to this recurrent and poignant demand, there always arises a plentiful supply of those who claim to meet it adequately. Most of these claimants are impostors.

—Meher Baba

There are three powers alone able to conquer and hold captive forever the conscience of these impotent rebels for their happiness—these forces are miracle, mystery, and authority.

—Doestoevsky's Inquisitor in *Brothers Karamazov*

5

Meeting Spiritual Shadow: Darkness on the Path

Sadly but inevitably, the longing for the light typically evokes its opposite: a shattering encounter with spiritual darkness, an emptying out of hope, meaning, and previous images of god. Our suffering hollows us out, tears at veils of spiritual persona, smashes religious idols, and ultimately leaves us bereft.

Before this encounter with spiritual shadow, we are, like Adam and Eve, faithful and trusting believers. We are the chosen; we will be saved; we can be enlightened; god is on our side.

We begin the journey in innocence, filled with a longing to be saved, awakened, healed, or simply to belong. We may find a cherished teacher or participate in a community and engage in religious ritual or spiritual practice. We may enjoy a sense of membership and moments of deep fulfillment, even rapture. We may experience ecstatic altered states of consciousness or simply a more quiet mind and compassionate heart.

But at some point we may meet the shadow of a spiritual authority, suffering blatant emotional or sexual abuse. Or we may feel the consequences of a series of small, insidious transgressions. Or we may uncover a coercive group dynamic that becomes intolerable. But, in any case, we see through the *imago* of an idealized priest or teacher to a dark shadow or human limitation, and our projection rattles. If the disappointment is deep, if the disillusionment is shattering, we enter the night sea journey, the Via Negativa, or way of darkness.

In the Christian mythos, this is the time of the cross. As we read in *Mark* 15:33: When the sixth hour came there was darkness over the whole land until the ninth hour. And at the ninth hour Jesus cried out in a loud voice, "My God, my God, why have you deserted me?"

At first, we may try to deny what we see in others. One disciple of a swami accused of abuse explained, "If I believed such stories, I would disbelieve my whole life. I have no room for such thoughts. I might doubt my own perception. I might doubt my own eyes. But I cannot doubt that strength which has given me everything."

In a different scenario, we deny our own shadows, those unconscious feelings and beliefs that are deemed unacceptable by our teachers and communities. But at some point, those hidden thoughts and feelings—a cynical, gnawing doubt, an intractable, inexplicable depression, a persistent, destructive habit—erupt into consciousness. Then one day we admit to ourselves that, despite our faith in a church or a teacher's promises, despite our diligence in our attendance or our practices, we still struggle with our own darkness. A spiritual life can't save us from suffering.

One man told me, "The more I meditated by day, the more I drank at night. At first, I didn't think anything of it because my parents drank, my brother drank, my teacher drank too. Taking it for granted, the drinking became invisible.

"Then someone pointed out that I couldn't get through an evening without drinking. Slowly, I began to realize that, yes, I was an alcoholic. And my teacher and my practices colluded with my problem."

In yet another scenario, our beliefs and rituals fail to fulfill on their promises. One Sufi told me that he practiced *zikhr,* or chanting the names of god, for 25 years. But he never felt a moment of transcendence or *fana.* Gradually, his faith in Sufism eroded, and he felt too demoralized to practice. A Christian Science practitioner reported that, after a remarkable healing years before, which lit the flame of faith, her prayers seemed to go unanswered. Serious symptoms of diabetes and financial problems plagued her, despite her practitioner's explanation that they were not real, but merely "claims" that god is not all-powerful. In the end, she turned to medicine for help and lost her faith.

If we strive for spiritual perfection, our practices inevitably fail us. And all too often this striving stems from emotional needs for approval and a relentless inner critic. Dominican scholar Matthew Fox has pointed out that believers who learn to trust creation see that beauty and imperfection go together both in nature and in the human body. Our imperfections unite us in vulnerability and lead to compassion for one another. But the ego's quest for perfection traps us isolation and in a longing that cannot be fulfilled.

Some yoga practitioners who yearn for that unattainable perfect body—strong, sculpted, and flexible—report that their *asana* practices reinforce their negative body images. Instead of finding calm and sanctuary from hatha yoga, they strived for a standard that left them feeling unattractive, ashamed, and not good enough.

One woman told me that she thought she left behind self-punishing behaviors and self-critical thoughts when she quit jogging, but later discovered that she brought them along to the yoga mat. Imposing grueling demands on her body and viewing it judgmentally from the outside, she maintained feelings of shame and failure. When she discovered that her yoga teacher was anorexic, she felt devastated and quit her practice.

I, too, suffered this kind of painful disillusionment with my practice: when meditators all around me reported psychic and subtle-level experiences, I simply sat, day after day, with a quiet mind: no lights, no visions, no voices, no rushes of energy. I began to wonder what was wrong with me. Or whether my nervous system was damaged. Or whether my psychic boundaries were impenetrable. Or whether I was doing the practice incorrectly. In the end, I wondered whether I was on the wrong path.

In addition, a recurrent social, psychological, or physical problem may be caused or exacerbated by the practice. In a private communication, psychologist Aaron Kipnis offered several examples: a college student attended an intensive weekend seminar on meditation and frequently began to miss school due to disorientation. A man used a repetitive chant to attempt to treat his anxiety but grew increasingly anxious when he failed to chant. Another isolated himself to meditate for longer and longer periods in order to withdraw from using drugs but suffered withdrawal symptoms when he stopped meditating. Each of these people became dependent on a spiritual technique, experienced subsequent problems with it, and was unable to reduce its use.

Finally, the abuse of power and sex among priests and Eastern teachers has brought about widespread demoralization, leading many people to question the purpose of religion and the goal of spiritual practice, once seen as the purpose of life itself. After all, Hindu teachings say that when the mind is established in transcendence, and we act from the highest level of awareness, we can perform only right action. And Buddhist teachings say that when the mind is cleansed of defilements, behavior will be liberated from greed, anger, and ignorance. How, then, do we make sense of abusive behaviors by celibate priests or allegedly realized teachers?

For many believers, enlightenment or Self-realization has been thrown into doubt. For them, the spiritual quest today looks more like mindful awareness in everyday life.

As Helen Tworkov pointed out in *Tricycle: The Buddhist Review* (Summer 1994), after many teacher scandals in the 1980s, Buddhist concerns shifted from awakening the mind to establishing ethical norms. However, she said, "ethical behavior may or may not be born of fundamental insight into the nature of reality. It may or may not be released through the compassion inherent in our Buddha-nature." If ethics are separated from realization, she wrote, then Buddhist ethics offers nothing new to a predominantly Christian society, which prescribes behavior based on scripture, rather than rooted in consciousness.

To sum up, we may meet a teacher's shadow, we may meet our own shadow, or we may suffer disillusioment with spiritual beliefs or practices. In any case, our dreams of transcendence and communion fade. We lose faith and fall from grace. We feel forsaken, even by god.

With the fall, some believers turn away from god, becoming bitter disbelievers who feel confused and disoriented with the fellowship of community and the guidance of doctrine. Others retrench against the threat of loss and defend the fortress of belief with louder right-and-wrong thinking. They attempt to ascend again, denying the meaning hidden in the fall. They rationalize their beliefs, excuse their abusive experiences at the hands of others, or trade in their spiritual props for another set, climbing back toward the heavens of naivete. Finally, others grab for the brass ring of a materialistic life.

Those few who turn to face the disillusionment and loss are, like Job, angry, betrayed, and empty-handed. As one client told me, "I didn't want to hear the rumors about my minister's behavior. For the longest time, I couldn't look at the abuse, like a blind spot. After all, my whole life was in the church. And if I questioned anything, I would be seen as a doubter, no, a heretic.

"Then, one day, something snapped: I needed to know. I no longer wanted to live in delusion.

"But the truth was devastating. How could this revered man commit such a travesty? Suddenly, nothing made sense. I had no reason to get out of bed in the morning."

When the meeting with the Other occurs, the descent begins. And it is this loss of innocence and descent to the underworld that initiates us into the mystery and complexity of human life, especially as it is linked to divine life.

Encountering the spiritual Other: the breakdown of communion

One of the first signs of a saint will be the fact that other people do not know what to make of him.

—Thomas Merton

The guru is a kind of irritation to his friends. You can't sleep with a dog barking in your ear. The guru is always annoying people with his demand to stay awake. Therefore, he doesn't satisfy the seeker. Those who come to be satisfied are offended.

—Da Love Ananda

In *The Anthropologist on Mars,* Oliver Sacks tells the following story, which he calls the Last Hippie: In Berkeley in the late sixties, a young student disappeared. When his parents last saw him he seemed to be healthy, thin and wiry, with a full head of hair. As time passed without word, they grew more frightened and finally hired a private detective to help. The young man was found on the east coast in a Hare Krishna commune.

Filled with hope and dread, his parents boarded a plan to visit. A swami in orange robes brought their son to the door. He was unrecognizable: obese, hairless, and lethargic. The parents were confused and bereft. What had happened to their only son?

The swami explained: their son was enlightened. He was imperturbable, living fully in the present moment and liking everyone equally.

Stunned, the parents asked if he had any health problems. He complained recently about dimming eyesight. But, the swami added, his physical sight was weakening because his inner sight was growing.

The parents were distraught. They insisted on taking their son to a nearby hospital for a battery of tests. Doctors soon discovered that he had a pituitary tumor the size of a grapefruit, which had grown into his frontal lobes and put pressure on his optic nerve. The tumor had progressed so far that it was no longer operable.

Appalled, the man's parents called in Oliver Sacks for a consultation, and he administered a range of neuropsychological tests. The man had no memory except for a small period in the 1960s. And what he remembered most were song lyrics by the Grateful Dead.

So, Sacks arranged to take him to a Dead concert. When the music began, the man leapt out of his wheelchair, alive and kicking. He sang along with every word of every song. But when the concert ended, he slumped back into the chair, dazed and lethargic, and returned to his former state.

Two days later, when Sacks visited him and asked how he enjoyed the concert, the man replied, "What concert?"

I tell this story to illustrate what I mean by spiritual abuse: a mistreatment in a religious setting that results in an injury to that which is central to soul—our faith. Spiritual abuse is a betrayal of trust by the people to whom we entrust our faith, those who carry a higher authority or an *imago dei.*

This kind of abuse may be covert, such as the misuse of spiritual understanding to rationalize events, which ends in neglect or another kind of harm. The Krishnas' spiritual frame led them to deny outside evidence of medical problems. They were blinded in the name of vision, overlooking bodily problems because they devalued them as unspiritual. They interpreted memory loss as living in the present moment, growing blindness as a gift. They did not intend harm; they simply denied or refused to see what was before them because they elevated everything to its highest common denominator—a spiritual reality.

Many traditions perpetrate covert abuse. A Hasidic teacher said he would offer me more teachings only if I kept the Sabbath and became kosher. A Christian Science practitioner told a woman that a major decision she made, which appeared to be mistaken, had to be correct because they had prayed about it. A Nicheren Shoshu Buddhist reported that when she stopped chanting, she grew depressed and was told her "low-life condition" stemmed from not chanting. A member of a small Hindu community reported that she gave her inheritance to the guru because he said that her financial advisor was not all-knowing, as he was. A man whose family belonged to Jehovah's Witnesses was discouraged from any outside education because, they said, Watchtower activities of going door to door held greater value. A Zen Buddhist woman told me that she left her feelings of doubt about the *roshi* at the door of the *zendo* in the name of right speech.

If human behavior is controlled by an external moral authority, and language is shaped by giving special meanings to words, believers internalize that control. Shame, guilt, and self-criticism, seeds planted in early childhood, are already in place to reinforce group norms. A devout Episcopalian high school student, kneeling on wooden benches, learned to repeat these prayers: "We do not presume to come to this thy table, o merciful Lord, trusting in our own righteousness, but in thy manifold and great mercies. We are not worthy so much as to gather up the crumbs under thy table. Have mercy upon us, miserable offenders."

When this same man later learned to meditate in his continuing quest for divine guidance, his teacher's shaming messages resonated with truth. He told me, "I'm not worthy of becoming enlightened. I need to meditate more, a lot more. If I question his authority, I might leave the group. Then I'll surely end up in a hell realm."

When demeaning and controlling messages are continually reinforced through lectures, pressures to conform, and punishments for aberrant thought or behavior, before long most of us submit. We lose the right relationship between self-worth and humility.

As the Self is projected onto a teacher, and group identity is cemented with a secret teaching that carries the light side of life, the dark side typically is projected outside of the group. In this way, enemy-making begins. We come to believe that the world is divided into the in-group (the pure, saved, enlightened ones) and the out-group (the impure, unsaved, ignorant ones, or heretics).

As projection of the collective shadow takes on a life of its own, the in-group identifies with moral superiority, and the out-group carries their inferiority and the traits that go with it—materialistic, hedonistic, or greedy. Those qualities that the community can't tolerate within it are unconsciously attributed to the enemy. With black-and-white thinking institutionalized, the nuances of shadow within the in-group and goodness within the out-group are lost. Self-righteousness is reinforced.

Eventually, the outsiders become foes, then scapegoats. In extremists groups, the enemy is ripe for sacrifice because it has been dehumanized, even demonized, no longer deserving of life. For that reason, those who kill them will be spiritually rewarded. Islamic fundamentalist suicide bombers believe, for example, that their violent acts assure them a place in paradise. In this way, the ultimate function of warring with an enemy becomes redemption.

In that context, the ends justify the means. We may begin by telling small lies to our families. (TM is a stress-reduction technique, not a spiritual practice.) We manipulate others to seduce them into joining us. (The Hare Krishnas call their deception "transcendental trickery." Jehovah's Witnesses call it "theocratic strategy.") And we come to value an abstract set of principles that gives us inner coherence and direction over human life. (Certain Christian groups believe that nuclear war is not a risk because, if it happens, they will be taken up into the rapture to join Christ in heaven.)

When a conflict arises between our feelings and our ideology, we are told and may come to believe that *we* are wrong. The doctrine is more valid than our direct experience. And our doubts merely point to our own weakness, lack of faith, past transgressions, or poor character. Therefore, we must change ourselves in order to tolerate any discrepancy.

This cognitive dissonance between what we feel, know, or see and what we are told by a religious authority figure can have a surprising result: apocalyptic groups that predicted the end of the world grew stronger after the prophecy failed. Needing to maintain meaning and reinforce their self-images as true believers, most members did not question or doubt their "truths," but defended them even more virulently.

The same phenomenon occurred within meditation groups: when practitioners did not become enlightened, as promised, many blamed themselves for being too neurotic and Western culture for being too stressful. The teacher and the practice were not responsible.

Robert Jay Lifton, who is well known for his study of thought reform in extremist groups, points out that any set of emotionally charged convictions about the human relationship to the divine can be carried to an extreme—when a community becomes a cult. From that point on, group mind takes hold, and there is little tolerance for doubt, ambiguity, or critique. Some communities prohibit contact with outsiders, prescribe rigorous training, and demand strict obedience. Eventually, members report that they feel powerless to leave and fear retaliation if they try.

Spiritual abuse also may be overt: money, power, and sexual shadows in religious teachers may lead to outright coercion or molestation. The international scandal of sexual abuses by Catholic clergy unfolded during the completion of this book. Hundreds of supposedly celibate priests in the U.S., the U.K, Ireland, Mexico, France, Austria, Poland, Hong Kong, and Nigeria were accused of adultery, teen, and child molestation. Their cardinals stand accused of knowing that pedophilia was taking place in their parishes, denying the accusations, transferring these priests to other communities, paying hush money to silence victims, engaging in retaliatory litigation, and failing to report the crimes to law enforcement.

As of January 2002, the Boston archdiocese had given prosecutors the names of 90 priests suspected of abuse. At least 84 others in eleven states were accused during the first few months of that year. Richard Sipe, author of *Sex, Priests, and Power*, estimated that nearly 50 percent of Catholic priests break their vows of celibacy.

A survey of evangelical ministers conducted by researchers at *Christianity Today* (1988) found that 12 percent of clergy admitted to having sex with someone other than a spouse. Twenty-three percent stated they had been sexually inappropriate with a non-spouse. A 1991 survey of Protestant pastors (by the Center for Ethics and Social Policy, Graduate theological Union, Berkeley) found that about 10 percent had been involved with a parishioner. And 70 percent of Southern Baptist respondents told the *Journal of Pastoral Care* (winter 1993) that they knew of pastors who had had sexual contact with congregants.

In the archdiocese of Chicago, a commission reviewed allegations of clergy abuse during the last 25 years and concluded that 39 priests—or five percent of all priests—had been validly accused. Although activists claim that as many as 70 priests should be charged, even the low estimate is shocking: if translated into national proportions, between 2,000 and 4,000 priests may be guilty of sexual abuse of children or minors.

The number of victims of any perpetrator varies. For example, in Boston more than 130 allegations have been made against now defrocked priest John Geoghan. Father Andrew Greeley suggested that, if we assume a conservative number of 50 victims for 2,500 priests, the victim population would exceed 100,000.

As of March 2002, the Catholic church had paid out between $600 million and $1.3 billion to victims of abuse. However, following large damage awards by juries, the church became wary of going to trial. As a result, in August 2001, it disclosed that it paid $5.2 million to an individual who claimed molestation by a priest. Although he denied the allegations, the priest agreed to apply to the Vatican to be removed from his status. (As of this writing, the Vatican does not grant U.S. bishops permission to dismiss perpetrators from the priesthood.)

Institutional changes, while slow in coming, have begun at last: In spring, 2002, the Pope summoned American cardinals to Rome to discuss pedophilia among the clergy and stated that those who were guilty had succumbed to the power of evil. He called the abuse of minors both a crime and a sin, signaling to bishops to cooperate with law enforcement. But he offered no concrete guidance for defrocking priests.

In June, the bishops agreed to remove priests who abused even one child in the past or any following the adoption of the new policy. They also agreed to report allegations to the civil authorities, relinquish confidentiality agreements in lawsuits, do background checks on those who work with children, and create a lay review board to examine accusations.

After a four-year legal battle and to prevent a jury trial, the Los Angeles and Orange County dioceses finally agreed to changes in their policy, including a one-strike provision, which dismisses a priest found guilty of a single incident of abuse. In addition, they will monitor parishes and schools, establish toll-free phone numbers and a website for anonymous complaints, teach abuse prevention at parochial schools, and forbid priests to be alone in social settings with minors. Rhode Island passed a ground-breaking law saying that priests must report what they learn of spiritual abuse in the confessional. The church has objected, saying that if bishops or priests become mandated reporters, like therapists who must tell police of crimes, others will not confide in them. And bowing to public pressure, Cardinal Bernard Law of Boston agreed to require clergy to report to authorities even past allegations of abuse by priests.

In addition, several difficult topics that were previously taboo have emerged in public discourse for the first time, although they remain tentative and limited as of this writing: the risks of a large number of homosexual Catholic priests, the risks of the culture of celibacy, and the risks of the absence of women in the priesthood. In addition, the role of lay church members, who are seeking a greater voice in policy-making, is under discussion.

One of the nation's leading Catholic magazines said that church hierarchy was incapable of investigating itself and that bishops had lost credibility. A March 2002 poll reported that 75 per cent of American Catholics believed that U.S. bishops were doing a "poor" or "fair" job in addressing the crisis. In particular, calls for the resignations of Cardinal Law of Boston and Cardinal Egan and of New York for their inaction and implicit collusion with abusers rang out across the country.

As a result, the Church climate is undergoing a sea change: the focus is no longer on a single disturbed priest but on the system that supported this behavior, covered it up, and forgave perpetrators without assurances that they had changed. If church policy toward misbehaving priests is to shift from individual sin and redemption to dismissal and punishment, the church will need to separate spiritual questions from legal and policy questions. It will need to redefine the zone of its moral concern. It will, in effect, need to undergo a Via Negativa—an encounter with the depths of its own darkness.

Responses to clergy sexual misconduct in other denominations have varied to date: the Episcopal Church has detailed policies and trainings on how to maintain personal boundaries, while the Southern Baptist Convention has none. Other Protestant denominations, especially those that ordain women, have begun to hold seminars on preventing abuse. The Central Conference of American Rabbis has guidelines on how to investigate, report, and adjudicate allegations of abuse. The Orthodox community, which was rocked by accusations in 2002 that a well-known youth official had been sexually abusing teens under his care, has begun to develop new policies.

Finally, scores of high-profile clergy have been accused of financial fraud and embezzlement. State regulators have warned of scams that play on religious loyalties to persuade people to mortgage homes or pull cash from retirement funds. According to a story in the Santa Barbara *News-Press* (August 8, 2001), regulators in 27 states have taken actions against individuals and companies that used religious beliefs to gain the trust of more than 90,000 investors, in some cases even kneeling to pray with their victims. Three big schemes involving the Baptist Foundation of Arizona, Greater Ministries International Church, and IRM Corporation, have cost investors 1.5 billion dollars.

Spiritual abuse is ecumenical: teachers of Eastern traditions have toppled from their pedestals too, leaving many communities in denial, despair, and disillusionment. Swami Rama, whose yogic powers, according to Elmer Green of the Meninger Foundation, included changing brain waves and stopping his heart at will and moving objects with his mind alone, offered inspiration and instruction to many about the vast range of human capacities. But in 1990 *Yoga Journal* reported that he had been having secret sexual affairs with female students for years. According to witnesses, he used his powers to discern their needs, cultivate their self-doubts, and coerce them into sexual obedience. For one, he promised a trip to India; for another, he disclosed they had been together in a past life.

In addition, female members reported that they donated their labor, sacrificed privacy, were constantly monitored, and were often subject to humiliation, such as kicking, shaming comments, and dismissive behaviors. In one case, he allegedly bragged to disciples that a woman would do whatever he told her, then put his dog's collar and leash around her neck and walked her back and forth. Because his disciples agreed that, in his enlightened state, he could cause no harm but only help others achieve liberation, they refused to hear complaints or investigate reports of abuse.

Sogyal Rinpoche gained popularity when he published *The Tibetan Book of Living and Dying*. But in 1995, a female follower filed a lawsuit claiming he told her that "in pleasing and offering herself to him, she would be helping to heal her family and attain spiritual enlightenment." She further alleged that he required her to perform "degrading acts to prove her complete devotion" and advised her to leave both her husband and therapist.

Da Free John aka Adi Da, an unconventional spiritual teacher, was charged in 1985 by a former devotee with involuntary servitude, physical and sexual abuse, and fraud. According to the *Marin Independent Journal* (April 3, 1985), others also accused him of brainwashing, drug abuse, sexual coercion, and intense shaming—in the name of spiritual development. Shortly after, he moved to the island of Fiji.

The Ananda Church of Self-Realization, which split off from Yogananda's community, became a well-known residential retreat in California in the 1970s. But in 1998, a jury decided that its leader, Swami Kriyananda, was guilty of fraud: he presented himself as a celibate despite sexual relations with women. Kriyananda responded that, although he kept the title of swami, he had renounced his vows of celibacy when he married in 1985. Following the outcome of the trial, he relinquished his position in the church and moved overseas.

One man told me that after twenty-five years of meditation practice, he was finally enjoying the kinds of spiritual experiences he had imagined, due to the guidance of Dr. Frederick Lenz aka Atmananda aka Zen master Rama. But, according to *New York Magazine* (July 20, 1998), Lenz also coerced his followers to engage in sex with him, take drugs, and undergo fasting and sleep deprivation to produce altered states of consciousness. Originally a follower of Sri Chinmoy, in 1980 Lenz said he had achieved *samadhi* and went out on his own, claiming yogic powers. His quirky teaching style included intellectual rants, all-night music raves, desert trips to observe the stars, and recommendations of "higher vibratory" movies and products.

Unlike Eastern gurus who proclaim celibacy and anti-materialism, Lenz was openly sexual and acquisitive. He pushed many of his students into computer careers and, once they were earning high salaries, charged high tuitions for his own classes. However, according to ex-devotees, he encouraged them to lie, cheat, and infiltrate organizations that he disliked.

In the 1990s, several female followers reported that Lenz fed them psychedelics and seduced them. In addition, one follower of Lenz, a dear friend of mine, died of a drug overdose after giving Lenz $100,000 donation.

Following the scandals, Lenz swallowed 150 valiums and walked off the end of his Long Island dock with a female follower, having promised her his guidance into a higher spiritual plane. She survived to tell the story.

Although many of my Los Angeles friends delighted in the benefits of his Insight Transformational Seminars, John-Roger aka J-R aka the Mystical Traveler, founder of the Movement of Spiritual Inner Awareness, has been accused of sexually seducing male followers under spiritual pretense, accumulating vast wealth despite a vow of poverty, and using his spiritual powers to elicit obedience. According to a Nov. 1, 1994 report in the Los Angeles *Times*, J-R denied the allegations.

In 1975, 1979, and 1982, married Japanese abbot Eido-roshi of the Zen Studies Society of New York was accused of seducing emotionally vulnerable women students. He denied the allegations. In 1983, Maezumi-Roshi, a married abbot, openly apologized for affairs with several female students and for his alcoholism, for which he sought treatment.

In 1983, the San Francisco Zen Center was torn apart when the married abbot, Richard Baker-Roshi, *dharma* heir of Suzuki-Roshi, was found to be having an affair with a student. As board members broke through their denial and began to explore their options, a net of other abuses, held together by secrecy and shunning, unraveled: fiscal irresponsibility (the abbot drove a new BMW and purchased expensive, antique meditation robes while the students, who worked long hours in the center businesses, lived on a small stipend); abuses of power (the cluster of businesses that made up Zen Center were incorporated in such a way that Baker-Roshi had sole decision-making power. In addition, he could legitimize his choices with the mantle of his teacher, as his sole heir); and breaking his vows to obey the precepts of Buddhism, including "do no harm." (Baker-Roshi left behind a trail of broken-hearted women, as well as a shocked and humiliated community.)

During the accusations and denials of misconduct, Baker Roshi resigned as abbot. The rift between him and the community has remained bitter for years, despite the work of counselors and consultants hired by Zen Center.

In a 1994 interview in *Tricycle* magazine, Baker Roshi admitted that his own insecurity and self-importance lay beneath his behavior. Although he had hundreds of students, he never claimed to be "teacher." In this way, he said, he avoided the responsibility for his position, including dealing with the projections and seeing his own flaws.

In an interview in *Common Boundary* (Sept. 1994), author Andrew Harvey discussed his guru/disciple relationship with Mother Meera, an Indian woman who claims to be an incarnation of the divine feminine. Harvey became Meera's spokesman through his books and lectures. But soon after he found a male partner, he claims that she turned against his homosexuality and told him either to be celibate or marry a woman and inform people that she transformed him into a heterosexual.

Several colleagues and clients have told me about how the teachings and practices of Bhagwan Shree Rajneesh aka Osho liberated them from emotional constraints and healed them of childhood wounds. Dancing wildly until they couldn't think, tasting the ecstasy of bliss, some devotees claim, even today, that their time with Rajneesh was the most valuable period of their lives. But many high-profile media reports have described how the Indian teacher allegedly coerced people into cathartic Tantric sex practices with anonymous partners and absconded with devotees' money to buy Rolls Royces and property worldwide.

As his empire grew, Rajneesh apparently developed a dependence on nitrous oxide, stored guns at his ashram, and became increasingly isolated. Eventually, he fell into paranoia, accusing his closest followers of murder, assault, and arson.

Chogyam Trungpa Rinpoche, a Tibetan exile and Oxford-educated Buddhist teacher who founded Naropa Institute in Boulder, became well-known for translating intricate ideas and elaborate contemplative disciplines for Westerners in his Shambhala trainings. In the Vajrayana tradition, he urged his followers to embrace and transform their passions, both dark and light. Apparently, he did the same: in the name of "crazy wisdom," which aims to stop the ordinary mind's flow of words and images and to reduce the ego, Trungpa hosted wild parties, had sexual liaisons with students, and spoke his mind frankly, regardless of consequences. He received students' prostrations while reeking of sake. According to followers, his erratic, daredevil behavior, including his alcoholism, forced them into a choice between doubt and confusion or total acceptance and submission.

Following in Trungpa's tradition of having multiple sexual partners among his students, his *dharma* heir, Osel Tendzin, reportedly slept with both men and women in his community. Tragically, he contracted the HIV virus but kept it a secret—and continued his unprotected sexual escapades, ultimately infecting the very people who had placed their spiritual lives in his hands.

In 1988 Osel Tendzin's community discovered that he had been infected for nearly three years. Several board members had known of his illness. So had his teacher, Trungpa. The crisis sent a jolt through the American Buddhist community. Suddenly, a tradition devoted to ending suffering looked just like a cult.

Swami Muktananda, a meditation master known as Baba, who founded Siddha Yoga Foundation, was an adept at transmitting *shakti* or spiritual energy to his devotees. Many followers claimed that, as a result of his look or touch, their kundalini was awakened and their spiritual lives quickened. However, late in life, Muktananda was accused of molesting teenage girls. According to a story in *CoEvolution Quarterly* (Winter 1983), Muktananda claimed life-long celibacy despite reports of frequent seductions under the pretext of tantric practice.

When a young woman complained about the guru's behavior to Gurumayi, an Indian woman who studied with Baba since the age of 18 and is now head of Siddha Yoga, the latter replied that people had told her about this behavior for years. But she did nothing. Other followers rationalized the news by telling themselves that he was not fully penetrating the girls, or not ejaculating, or offering them a privileged initiation.

As the charges continued to mount, a Siddha Yoga swami wrote an open letter to Baba to make the accusations public. Baba denied the charges, while some devotees gave them spiritual explanations, and others left the fold.

Other witnesses reported that Baba beat people, permitted guns into the ashram, and used strong-arm tactics to bring errant followers into line. One young man was allegedly stripped, put under a cold shower, and beaten with a rubber hose. Devotees rationalized these behaviors as ego reductions, much like Zen masters who hit their students with a stick to stop their busy minds.

Gurumayi, who now oversees 550 meditation centers and ten ashrams around the world, is beloved by tens of thousands of people. But she also has been embroiled in controversy. An article in the *New Yorker* (Nov. 14, 1994) described her bitter family feud with her brother to take over the organization after Muktananda's death in 1982, when she was 27 and he was 19. In 1985, she told devotees to destroy photos and videos of her brother, Nityananda, because his time as successor to Baba was up. He was accused of breaking his vow of celibacy, and he admitted his transgressions.

Later that year, in India, Nityananda told the *New Yorker* that his sister locked him up, stripped him of his status and his name, forced him to cede access to funds left to him by Baba, and installed herself as sole successor. Days later, Gurumayi appeared with several women, who allegedly struck him with bamboo canes for three hours. When asked, Gurumayi confirmed the isolation and caning of her brother. Rumors of her own affair with a close official have been unsubstantiated. But anyone who visits Nityananda for spiritual teaching to this day faces potential threats and certain banishment from Siddha Yoga.

In the company of many teachers, students describe euphoric states and spiritual breakthroughs, as well as suffering due to sexual, emotional, or financial coercion. They say that their awe often left them incapable of true consent. For many, the blessings were so precious that it feels almost sinful to point out the curses. If he or she does such and such, they say, it means nothing in the context of his gift to humanity.

But others become so distressed by insidious breaches of trust that their early childhood wounds resurface, their capacity for trust breaks, and their faith in others, in themselves, and in a higher order erodes.

The consequences of spiritual abuse

This spectacle of corrupt priests and teachers in authoritarian communities has cast a pall over religion and spirituality. To cynics, it's a soap opera of charlatans and fools, villains and victims. Their holy longing buried beneath more socially acceptable desires, they cannot understand why anyone would place their highest value on a church, a teacher, or a practice that claims a connection with the divine.

But I suggest that the situation is much more complex: while media sensationalism reinforces widespread suspicion of our religious desires, men and women in every tradition continue to have authentic spiritual breakthroughs. When they taste transcendence or stabilize higher levels of consciousness, they may come to believe that they are then prepared to preach or teach or hold *satsang*. However, a glimpse of awakening—*kensho, samadhi*, or *satori*—does not prepare a person to teach. It does not mean he or she can handle the complexities of guiding others, especially others with diverse psychologies from diverse cultures. If a teacher is charismatic or develops special powers but has not completed ego- and shadow-work, his or her effects will be mixed: transmission of knowledge with resulting gratitude among students, alongside transmission of shadow with resulting devastation.

In addition, a religious or spiritual leader may have high development along the spiritual line, including deity mysticism or union with spirit, but low growth along the moral line. For this reason, we have seen clearly wise people act as if they are unaware of the painful consequences of their behavior on others.

Following the shock and disillusionment that believers feel after meeting the spiritual shadow, some succumb to rage, blaming the church or *satsang*, the teacher, god, or themselves. Their feelings of broken trust and spiritual betrayal lead them to distrust others and to lose faith.

Others succumb to depression. All at once, they lose their community, their purpose, and the meaning that bound their lives together. They regret the time they dedicated to their practices or teachers. Many feel guilty about the lies or deceptions with which they colluded. Others feel ashamed at having been duped or used by a charismatic teacher or priest. They struggle with loneliness, sexuality, finances, and other developmental issues that were delayed by living within an authoritarian setting. And they fear retaliation for separating from the group, whether it takes the form of physical, emotional, or spiritual punishment.

If their daily lives were organized by others and if their beliefs were prescribed by others, they may suddenly find themselves passive or indecisive. Unable to heed the cues of their own feelings and instincts, they may be dependent on obeying an outside authority. If they habituated to hours of prayer, chanting, or meditation, they may continue to slip into trance-like states or episodes of "floating," in which it's difficult to concentrate or remain in the present moment.

When sexual violations are involved, the consequences can be severe. At the March 1998 California Psychological Association conference in Los Angeles, Nanette de Fuentes likened sexual activity between a priest and parishioner to incest. It begins in a context of closeness. The priest is protected from suspicion by his role. The victim, who has an emotional attachment to him, is disbelieved because of the priest's authority. Or she is disbelieved because of the myth of the seductive woman, whose evil nature coerces the man. Her silence is obtained through threats. And she is responsible, through her secrecy, for maintaining his public image and the image of the church.

And, in the case of child abuse, the loss of trust and innocence are accompanied by the loss of self. Experts suggest that the closer the relation to the offender, the greater the trauma to the child. Most suffer post-traumatic stress symptoms, such as elevated arousal, sleep disturbances, deep distrust, sexualized behaviors, chronic depression, eating disorders, substance abuse, and suicidal thoughts. A survey in the *Journal of Social Issues* (51:2) reported that almost 20 percent of children abused by religious authorities subsequently consider suicide.

David Clohessy, a survivor of clergy abuse and member of the Survivors Network of Those Abused by Priests in Chicago, described the resulting shift in perception for him: "It's like getting up one morning, walking outside, and all of a sudden the law of gravity isn't in effect anymore. It is something that is so far beyond the pale of expectation for a kid ... It is just a horrible, horrible betrayal." (*Common Boundary,* Nov./Dec. 1996).

I would make another link: children often see their clergy as god. Developmentally, they may be unable to distinguish the human being from the *imago dei.* For that very reason, they are vulnerable to being told that the abusive behavior is "god's gift" or "god's punishment." And, for that same reason, they cannot distinguish between a person's behavior and an entire tradition of faith. Because the one they turn to for safety is the one who betrays them, they often give up their spiritual desires or try to submerge their religious yearnings altogether.

But the results of spiritual membership are not all negative. Many students also report more complex consequences than the media acknowledges, especially the anti-cult press, which demonizes alternative communities. Several disillusioned believers told me that, in retrospect, they see how they needed to break away from their families, especially an authoritarian parent, and used their spiritual families to do so. They longed for a parent *imago* or they longed for home, where they would be taken care of. That is, a younger part of them, perhaps a child part, needed to fulfill its unmet needs for dependency.

In *The Wrong Way Home*, Arthur Deikman called this hidden motivation covert dependency—the wish for parents and the parallel wish to be loved, admired, and sheltered by a group. This longing, he said, generates a hidden fantasy that can transform a priest or teacher into a parent and a fellowship group into a family. The result: we feel secure at last.

One client reported that the sense of belonging and kinship she felt at her church helped to heal the loneliness and alienation she felt in her family. However, her daughter, who was raised in that church, needed to separate from it and look elsewhere in search of her own identity. A man, who was raised as a secular Jew in an enmeshed, controlling family, became Orthodox in his twenties. His family was just as outraged at his religiosity as they would have been if he had converted to Catholicism or Islam. And in that way he made his separation.

Author Andrew Harvey has said that his guru/disciple relationship with Mother Meera mirrored his tie to his own mother: like Meera, his mother would appear briefly, enchanting and magnanimous, and then depart, leaving him wanting more. So, he recreated the early dynamic in an unconscious effort to heal it.

Jung made this point many years ago when he suggested that a "secret society" could be used as an intermediary stage on the way to individuation. However, while we may use a group identity, such as a religious or spiritual community, to differentiate from another group, such as a family, we risk losing our autonomy to belong to any collective. Therefore, for Jung, this is only a temporary solution: our psychological task is really to differentiate ourselves from others and stand on our own feet. From that point of view, all collective identities are transitional and, at some point, interfere with individuation.

But before many members are able to separate, they may fulfill early developmental needs and gain deeper meaning and purpose, which had not been provided by their childhood religions, material pursuits, or political activism. Long-term meditators may learn to discipline and empty their minds. A few gain peak states, their restless yearning satiated for a time. And a select few establish a new level of consciousness.

But most also point to the emotional damage they suffered at the hands of a priest or guru or coercive group dynamic. As one woman said, "I trusted completely, and that trust was betrayed. I was vulnerable, and that vulnerability was misused. Whatever innocence I had when I arrived, I lost. I created pain for people I loved and postponed finding real solutions for how to build an adult life, trading away precious time for a solution that wasn't a solution. In short, I paid dearly for the riches I gained."

Uncovering patterns of abuse

The light of perfection brings imperfection to the surface.

—Sufi proverb

When we first approach a guru, we should carefully examine his qualities and his actions. He should have conquered desire and anger and banished infatuation from his heart.

—Swami Muktananda

Spiritual growth is about surrender, not understanding. Whenever that part of you that wants to figure out, or know why, or know what for kicks in, kick it out.

—Swami Chetanananda

When examined together, the incidents of spiritual abuse cited above reveal patterns across denominations. The priest/parishioner, teacher/student relationship can be the most sacred of a lifetime. We invest it with the vision of our highest human potential; we entrust it with soul. Yet we are reluctant to find fault and to admit violations of trust because of that very investment. If the relationship fails, it invalidates not only our own judgment, but the very vision to which we devoted our lives. For this reason, denial is epidemic.

As one woman wrote in *The Promise of Paradise,* a book about her life at Rajneesh's Oregon community, "Before Rajneeshpuram, I could never understand how so many Jews stayed put during Hitler's ascent. But now I was witness to my own astonishing ability to rationalize away what I didn't want to face."

When victims finally acknowledge their own experiences of religious abuse, their communities often refuse to validate them. The Catholic priesthood has behaved for decades like a tribal brotherhood, protecting its own from charges of abuse by the laity. In Hindu groups, victims' complaints are devalued as "purification" (the elimination of toxic feelings or energies due to practice), in Buddhist *sanghas* as "deluded mind," and in Christian Science as "mortal mind" (the limited human mind that believes it's separate from god). Few religious or spiritual groups provide procedures to voice unacceptable thoughts and feelings in a nonjudgmental setting.

Other members often may blame the victim for being seductive, destabilizing the community, or endangering the higher good to humanity that the teacher offers. When a client's closest friends in her *sangha* refused to hear her doubts and turned their backs, she experienced a secondary trauma, the loss of precious friendships, cultivated over many years, which she expected to endure beyond her relationship to the teacher. When a Jehovah's Witness client began to express doubt, he was told that non-witnesses are "bad association" and if he spoke with them he would be "disfellowshipped," or expelled.

Although a group's teachings may be valuable and rituals or practices life-enhancing, an organization's structures may be authoritarian and its members' behavior patterns compulsive and cult-like. In fact, the coping strategies that are epidemic in alcoholic homes are prevalent in churches and spiritual communities:

- A priest or teacher, like a parent, exploits others for his or her own narcissistic needs. ("Thinking I had some extraordinary means of protection, I went ahead with my business as if something would take care of it for me," Vajrayana Buddhist teacher Osel Tendzin admitted after he had infected several followers with the HIV virus.)

- The teacher's transgressions are often boundary violations, whether psychic, emotional, sexual, or financial. (A follower of Chetanananda feared him because she believed that he could read her mind after staring into her eyes during meditation for years.)

- Like a child, the member chosen for abuse is made to feel special. (A follower of Frederick Lenz or Rama said, "I worked as his housekeeper for a year, cleaning and doing secretarial stuff for no pay. He had other girls over all the time. It made me jealous, but at the end of the day, I was the one who was in the same house.")

- Students and staff, like children, enable the teacher's dysfunctional behavior. ("We were all co-alcoholics," said a follower of Maezumi-roshi. "We in subtle ways encouraged his alcoholism because when he was drunk he would become piercingly honest.")

- Members deny their own feelings of doubt, danger, and common sense. ("That's hearsay. It's destructive to feed negative thoughts," said one Zen student on hearing about Richard Baker-roshi's affairs.)

- They project their ideal onto a priest or teacher, leading to psychological dependency. And they maintain that image at all costs, like a child protecting an abusive parent. (A Catholic told me, "Because he represents the church, he could not have abused her. She must have seduced him.")

- They rationalize destructive behavior as sanctioned by god or the lineage holder, or as a sacred teaching, or as "crazy wisdom," designed to startle the mind out of its conventional trance. (A Hindu meditator said, "When our teacher was late or failed to meditate or behaved rudely, we called it grist for the mill.")

- Shameful secrets hold the system together. (When Trungpa Rinpoche suffered dementia due to alcoholism, some devotees suggested that he was communicating with spiritual beings called *dakinis*. When he died at 47, only a few followers knew it was from the effects of alcoholism. The rest were not told or denied that his body could succumb to drink like that of an ordinary man.)

- Members are threatened with retaliation when they try to disclose secrets or wish to leave. ("My priest told me that if I revealed our secret, I would go straight to hell.")

Like many adult children of alcoholics, spiritual believers learn that their feelings don't matter because an authority figure knows them better than they know themselves. Therefore, self-knowledge originating from feelings or intuition is stigmatized, and we give up our capacity to discriminate based on our guts or our conscience. In effect, we give up self-trust.

One teacher publicly urged her followers to find their inner guru and become more self-reliant. But, in private, when a student expressed her uncertainty about a doctrine, the teacher responded, "When you look for the guru within, you only end up finding your own *samskaras*, those left-over impressions from the past that can be mistaken for directions from the superconscious. I've already charted this path. You're better off following me."

Episcopal priest Leo Booth, author of *When God Becomes a Drug*, believes that religious addiction is akin to alcoholism. In the early stages, he wrote, we use the Bible, prayer, or church attendance for their calming effects. Gradually, we begin to use them to avoid facing problems and to deal with uncertainty. As black and white thinking increases ("Sex is dirty, women are evil, non-believers are doomed"), we lose the capacity to think critically or question clerical authority. We begin to think compulsively about god, to quote scripture in every situation. Slowly, rationalization begins as we defend church attendance over all other duties, feel guilty if we miss it, and proselytize friends and family members.

As we lose other interests, we tithe more and more money to the church. We may undergo excessive fasting and develop an eating disorder. Eventually, we become isolated from people who think differently, avoiding nonreligious friends. In extreme cases, we may go on a crusade or mission to save the world.

One man had a mystical experience during prayer at a Pentecostal church. He began to fast weekly, read the Bible daily, and stop all of his recreational activities. He continued fasting for longer periods because he felt he wasn't spiritual enough. He lived in a car so that he could donate his rent money to the church. The pastor, who required his members to sign a form agreeing to abide by his "holiness standard," urged them to go out and win souls. This man bought a billboard to advertize the church.

Slowly and gradually, he realized that he could never do enough for the demanding god of his pastor. Rather than feeling at peace, he felt nagging guilt and shame. He began to question church policies and, as a result, the pastor spread rumors about him. His girlfriend abandoned him, and he plunged into depression, the scapegoat of his community.

With spiritual shadow-work, this man came to realize that the pastor's abusive behavior repeated the pattern of abuse by his father who, during alcoholic binges, criticized and humiliated him. As a boy, he internalized his father's name-calling and shaming messages, hoping against hope that one day, if he submitted, he would win his father's approval. In his relationship to the pastor, then, he was that young boy again, unconsciously seeking his father's approval, which rendered him powerless against the abuse. His next step: to create a conscious relationship to the holy as an adult with an internal sense of authority.

It seems to me that we can substitute the language of any tradition or practice for Father Leo's Christian terminology to discover whether we are using it compulsively and therefore have lost our ability to think critically and to choose it or not. For example, when I began meditation, I found its calming effect refreshing and rejuvenating. I looked forward each morning and evening to quieting my mind and relaxing my body. Gradually, I began to avoid stressful or challenging situations in order to enhance my practice. I meditated for longer periods and worked, played, and exercised for shorter ones. If I missed a session, I felt terrible guilt.

The meditation philosophy seemed to answer all of my philosophical questions. I felt sorry for those who hadn't found it. I began to use meditation and my beliefs to screen out potential love interests and friends. (To this day, my oldest friend tells me that I nearly lost her with my self-righteous prosceletyzing.) Practice became more important than relationship and career—no contest. I spent nearly ten years teaching meditation around the country with the certain knowledge that, the more meditators there were, the more chance for world peace. Today that naivete astounds me.

These transgressions by individual clergy and spiritual teachers, even those deemed "perfect masters," reveal that they are not immune to neurotic traits or shadowy behaviors. The attainment of mystical states or psychic and subtle levels of consciousness among saints and sages clearly does not mean that they fully transcend the ego. It does not do away with the personal history, personality, or temperament of the individual. However, in some cases, it may mean that they no longer identify with it. They no longer try to fulfill its needs.

And, just as clearly, it does not mean that they fully transcend the shadow or become aware of all of their disowned unconscious material. Although some teachers have suggested that a sudden moment of awakening illuminates all residue in the personal shadow, I no longer believe this possibility. Even if emotional and cultural shadow-work are an intentional, ongoing part of an individual's practice, the shadow still remains intact, at least in part, when one attains higher levels of awareness. In the end, I believe, we continue to banish material into the personal unconscious and to form shadow content at each moment because we are by nature unable to be aware of everything at once.

Hindus have a word for this phenomenon: *l'aish avidya*, or the remains of ignorance. Others have called it a phantom ego. In an article in my anthology *Meeting the Shadow*, Georg Feuerstein suggested that a phantom shadow may coexist with the phantom ego, permitting people at higher levels of consciousness to operate in conditional reality even after awakening to universal reality.

There is a Jewish teaching about this phenomenon: each human being has an evil inclination, or *yetzer harah*. This inclination does not disappear as a person evolves but, instead, grows stronger. The more light, the more darkness.

Feuerstein pointed out that the authoritarian style of most religious teachers does not permit them to use their followers as mirrors for their own development, which would enable them to do their own shadow-work or consciously wrestle with their *yetzer harah*. Instead, their vertical image of transcendence—their emphases on the "up" path only—leads them to ignore concerns about integrating personality and shadow. Therefore, they tend to remain authoritarian, idiosyncratic, and even abusive.

But individual explanations do not suffice to explain the epidemic of religious spiritual abuse. Vast cultural differences lie hidden beneath spiritual abuses as well. Ancient practices that evolved in specific contexts have been introduced to us with no supporting cultural contexts and very different unconscious organizations of reality. And, if waking up includes becoming aware of our invisible social and cultural conditioning, then we need to recognize those values, both conscious and unconscious, that we bring to our practices and those that we receive from them.

For example, our great emphasis on the value of the individual in the West does not exist in the East. In Japanese, there is not even a word for "individual." So, the pressing needs of Americans for attention, self-expression, and privacy may go unnoticed by Asian teachers who emphasize group mind or collective interests. And when students articulate these needs, they may be devalued.

At the same time, our conscious stress on individuality has a shadow side: unconsciously we may be drawn to groups that encourage *participation mystique*, or the loss of self, in the collective. In this way, the burden of heroic individualism—emotional, financial, and intellectual autonomy and creative achievement—can be lightened, which is what many members of spiritual communities report. ("When I surrender to the guru's grace, I don't have to strive so hard. When I feel belonging in the *sangha*, I don't have to face my isolation," a woman told me.)

The striving for success also can be relieved by teachings concerning the nature of the self. If the ego or self is an illusion, why try so hard to develop it or defend it? Why struggle to have a voice or protect ones boundaries? I can recall the great relief I felt when I believed that I needed to do nothing but meditate in order to feel worthy and to contribute to the well-being of others.

On the other hand, I have observed how the striving for material success can be displaced onto the striving for higher consciousness. That is, in some communities success comes to be equated with acquisition of spiritual experiences. And, conversely, failure is equated with prayer or meditation without results. As one Zen student said when asked why he no longer meditates, "Because my only association with *zazen* is of personal failure."

Our Western emphasis on individual empowerment and its anti-authoritarian bias also do not exist in the East. Instead, many Eastern spiritual communities are hierarchical, patriarchal, and feudal in their design. But an unconscious or shadow part of us longs to surrender to authority. So, that part of us fits with those institutional structures.

In addition, our emphasis on individual freedom and license collided with the East's emphasis on obedience and celibacy. Most Eastern methods of meditation evolved in monastic settings, which included abstinence from drugs, alcohol, and sex. Transplanted to America, which is obsessed with sex while condeming it as unspiritual, even sinful, these practices have been used to avoid intimacy and deny sexual problems.

Uprooted from their cultural foundations, some Eastern teachers acted out new-found freedoms with sex, money, and power in destructive ways. For instance, Trungpa Rinpoche was granted power in his teens, but his freedom was proscribed by collective medieval mores (such as concepts of communal pollution and purification) and cultural duties. Freed of restraints, he ran amok. Rooted in the same feudal Tibetan culture, Sogyal Rinpoche learned as a boy that a girl who became his sexual partner was blessed (in part because she left behind a life of poverty), and her family was blessed (because they were freed from supporting her and might receive gifts from the lama).

Conversely, some western practitioners have tried to adopt celibacy, abstinence, and gestures of subservience, such as prostrations. It's as if both teachers and disciples are acting out cultural shadows.

While Western culture is primarily guilt-based, the East is shame-based. In Asia, the need to save face overrides any ideas about open exchange or communication. For instance, the late lama Kalu Rinpoche, a wise and compassionate teacher, forbade his students from commenting on the behavior of Tibetan Buddhist teacher Osel Tendzin, who infected students with HIV. The appearance of harmony was more important to him than the expression of personal feelings or the enforcement of ethics.

The lack of ritual in our society also leads many of us to crave it. The slow, orderly, elegant rhythm of ceremony is an antidote to the rushed, chaotic, arbitrariness of our lives. But the risk of overvaluing ritual is that we lose ourselves in ancient, esoteric forms. Katy Butler reported in *CoEvolution Quarterly* (Winter 1983) that the atmosphere at San Francisco Zen Center was like a medieval palace, where rules for how to stand, bow, and sit were carefully prescribed.

One day, as Butler bowed repeatedly with other Zen students while the *roshi's* car departed, she saw herself—and felt stunned at her own behavior. "The day I stood there in front of that car, I was doing something I didn't understand, taking on Japanese behavior simply because I had been asked to." Butler realized later that the Japanese rituals at Zen Center had become a way of avoiding human contact.

Finally, the most obvious cultural gap is the gender gap. In Catholicism, Orthodox Judaism, and Islam, in which women cannot be ordained, patriarchal and authoritarian institutions remain calcified. In some Protestant denominations and Reform Judaism, which now ordain women, services and scriptures have been reimagined as less biased and more inclusive.

Historically, in the East, men and women have done spiritual practices separately and women could not be ordained. Some traditions also teach that women cannot become enlightened. Zen priest Yvonne Rand tells a story about visiting Japan while she was president of San Francisco Zen Center. With every meeting, she was introduced as wife of the president. Her Japanese peers could not even imagine a woman in her position.

Around the world, women have strived to throw off patriarchal forms of disempowerment and to find our voices, especially our valid anger. Therefore, these ancient beliefs and practices seem like a throw-back. However, according to Demaris Wehr, researchers found that many women still suffer a double-bind when trying to claim our own authority. Women who are authoritative are perceived as non-feminine. But more traditionally feminine women are perceived as childlike. Therefore, our ease with projecting our spiritual authority onto men and our difficulty with carrying it for ourselves has a cultural foundation.

In a personal communication, Wehr pointed to the example of Jessica Hahn, who was widely condemned for her affair with television evangelist Jim Bakker. But Hahn was raised with a theology of submission. She was taught that to submit herself to male authority was to submit herself to god. In other words, she was trained to accept exploitative behavior by male clergy. For such a woman to contradict a man is to contradict god. For such a woman to claim her own authority is to go against god. As Wehr concluded, she is made incapable of moral outrage on her own behalf.

Who is susceptible to spiritual abuse?

Although many people wrestle with holy longing, those with certain personal and family histories may be more susceptible to spiritual abuse. In the 1970s, when many Westerners turned East, the social and political aspirations of the 1960s had begun to fade. Like me, many seekers looked inward with the hope of transforming ourselves rather than our world—or transforming ourselves on the way to transforming our world. When we felt a gap between our actuality and our potential, our holy longing was stirred.

In a study reported in 1992 (in the *British Journal of Social Psychology*, vol. 30), researchers found that happiness occurs when we live our ideal images of ourselves. That is, when we experience our ideal self, as we do during heightened states of awareness or communal spiritual experience, we find the deepest satisfaction. The gap is closed between what is and what's possible. On the other hand, when there is a wide gulf between our reality and our ideal, the researchers found, we are most vulnerable.

Other research has shown that certain life turning points leave us susceptible to propaganda or religious conversion and to spiritual abuse: leaving home for the first time, entering the workplace after college, and facing the loss or death of a loved one. In other words, during key transitions we are open to shifts in meaning and purpose, which leaves us open to conversion, finding a new teacher or teaching.

I would add that certain personality styles and developmental issues make us vulnerable as well. A dependent style leaves us open to identifying with authoritarian leaders, who appear to play out our passionate but unconscious fantasies, whether they involve creating world peace or destroying America. Obsessive compulsive disorders may find a place in ritualized routine. Narcissism fits with an emphasis on self-involvement and feelings of specialness. And borderline disorders make believers susceptible to over-idealizing others, merging with them to hide from their own shameful inferiority, and filling their sense of emptiness with dogma. Trapped in a world of projections, those with borderline traits may distort reality by disowning their own shadows and creating scapegoats to carry their darkness for them. In addition, they suffer from a deep fear of abandonment and annihilation, which keeps them obedient and submissive until they feel betrayed, when they tend to retaliate with little concern for themselves or others.

In addition, the results of early sexual molestation—feelings of shame, especially about the body, porous psychic boundaries, anxiety, depression, and a tendency toward dissociation—leave students open to the allure of charismatic teachers. Feeling fundamentally flawed, survivors of sexual abuse may seek to become healed by association. Due to their unmet longings, their shadows lead them to project healer or savior onto a teacher, end up in a cult-like trance, and unconsciously repeat their early abusive experiences with their spiritual fathers.

Men and women who are caught in the archetype of the *puer aeternus*, or eternal youth, also are drawn to the high ideals of spirituality—and typically avoid the shadow. To others, they appear childlike and naïve, especially overtrusting. Rollo May called this trait "pseudoinnocence" and described it as the inability to see human destructiveness, which leaves one susceptible to others' shadows.

Granted a feeling of specialness by parents, which often covers over an inner emptiness, *puers* may lose their connection to the body and to earth. Unconsciously identified with the Self, they may become inflated. Chosen by an admired teacher, they feel special, as they did in childhood. As a result, the shadow is split off from the Self, and they long for the light.

Or they project the Self onto a teacher or savior. But in either case, the Self remains unstable, childlike and vulnerable. It's not tempered by suffering but instead seeks to maintain its grandiosity, avoid frustration, and overcome limits through spiritual experience. In this way, they seek a religious or spiritual solution to a psychological problem.

Religious and spiritual leaders are vulnerable to becoming perpetrators of abuse for parallel reasons. As a target of these powerful arrows of projection, which idealize him, a religious guide may feel his unfulfilled needs for admiration and mirroring being met by his followers. If he has disowned his inferiority, he may project it onto a student or a whole population and feel superior, as if he is a savior. Slowly, he may come to believe that he is the center of the universe.

After an assassination attempt on Pope John Paul II, for example, his sense of election became evident: he stated that he believed the Virgin Mary had altered the flight path of the bullet intended for him because he was put in his position and kept there by divine providence. At a feast for the Lady of Fatima, he placed the bullet on a statue of her.

If the devotion and selfless service of a teacher's followers lead him or her to feel invested in his position, he may unknowingly begin to enact their expectations of him. Like a romantic couple that is unconsciously living out each other's projections in order to receive love, the religious guide and his believers may unknowingly lose their individual separateness and become snared in a *folie a deux*. Instead of the freedom to shine as he is, the teacher may unconsciously feel pressure to fulfill the student's pictures of the *imago dei*, just as the students unknowingly attempt to fulfill the teacher's images of the dutiful follower.

If a teacher in this situation becomes isolated from peer feedback while he is banishing into the shadow those feelings and behaviors that don't fit his idealized image, he becomes cut off from his own vulnerability and from the opportunity to learn from his mistakes. As a result, he may succumb to identifying with the *imago dei*—ultimately believing himself to be so special that he's immune to the consequences of his actions, even immune to the HIV virus, as in the case of Osel Tendzin.

In this way, a religious teacher's isolation can have disastrous consequences, including sexual ones. In a 1985 *Yoga Journal* article, Buddhist meditation teacher Jack Kornfield described the results of interviews with 54 spiritual teachers of all traditions about their sexual activity. Only 15 actually remained celibate. Thirty-four of the 39 others had sexual liaisons with students. Their motivation, Kornfield said, was not always abuse of power. They yearned to step out of the isolation of their roles and, I would add, out of the isolation of carrying their students' projections.

In a psychotherapeutic relationship, the same danger arises with the client's transference onto the therapist, who carries both parental and god-like projections. With good training, a therapist aims to carry the projection knowingly, then hand it back at the proper moment, so that, in the end, the client can reclaim the power bestowed on the cherished Other.

However, this therapeutic ideal has been violated by countless professionals who have taken emotional, financial, and sexual advantage of their patients while succumbing to their own omnipotent fantasies. In California, an ongoing list of these violators is published regularly in professional journals, much like the posting of a Scarlet Letter.

Before I became a therapist, this risk seemed remote and difficult to understand. We simply know, rationally, that this is unethical and destructive behavior, so we "just say no." However, in a few brief moments when I have caught the arrow of a projected ideal and felt myself expand into it, I experienced the risk: instantaneously I *wanted* to be seen that way; I *wanted* to be loved that way; the power brought a heady rush. It could, for a moment, make me forget my own flaws.

As a veteran of shadow-work, I recognized that, in those moments, my power shadow colluded with a client's feeling of powerlessness or dependency. Like Peter Pan's Wendy, I began to stitch back my own shadow by recalling my wounds and limitations and embracing my basic humanity. Instead of feeling the loss of inflation, I breathed a sigh of relief.

Clergy and spiritual leaders also are at risk of perpetrating abuse if they suffer from untreated emotional problems, such as early traumas of abuse and abandonment, sexual compulsions, deep-seated narcissism, or alcohol and drug addictions, all of which tend to go unacknowledged because of their position or presumed level of consciousness. These emotional issues tend to reappear—a need to control, a contempt for weakness, a tendency for grandiosity—and become enshrined in the group.

Osama bin Laden is a case in point. The son of a Yemeni man who moved to Saudi Arabia and a concubine, who was either Palestinian or Syrian, he was an outsider from birth. In addition, he was neglected by his father, who had many wives and children, and then abandoned when his father was killed in the U.S. when Osama was ten. In college he visited nightclubs and bars, drank alcohol, and got involved with women. Eventually, overcome with guilt about indulging his own needs and desires, he turned to fundamentalist Islam and a longing for the father/god. When the West discovered him, he lived in a cave with four wives, fifteen children, and no running water.

All of those qualities that were banished into his shadow—personal desire, materialism, freedom of expression—were projected onto the infidels, especially Americans and Jews. And those traits that remained conscious in his persona—self-denial, asceticism, single-mindedness, self-righteousness—became enshrined among his followers.

James Gordon, author of *Golden Guru*, also pointed out this correlation between the guru's shadow and the ideal of the group. For instance, in his autobiography Rajneesh wrote that he decided at age six or seven, with his grandfather's death, not to let anyone become close to him. That is, he banished his dependency needs into the shadow. He fulfilled this vow in his later isolation, as well as in his admonition to devotees to remain emotionally unattached to others, even while being sexually intimate.

We can detect each other's shadows by noticing what we criticize in others. When a religious teacher accuses others of moral failings, then begins to fall into the same behaviors that he deems wrong, he is at risk of abuse. For example, in his last few years, Rajneesh fell into the same traps that he criticized in priests and politicians: he grew intoxicated with power, retaliated harshly against opponents, and used women to do his bidding because of their emotional loyalty.

Resesarch into human development during the past few decades sheds another light on what leaves students and teachers susceptible to receiving or perpetrating abuse. People do not develop all of a piece, with all of their traits moving forward in lock step. Rather, there are multiple lines of development or multiple intelligences—cognitive, emotional, psychosexual, aesthetic, moral, kinesthetic, spiritual—that appear to grow in independent ways. And the hierarchical levels of development, discussed above, appear in a particular developmental line. (Thanks again to Ken Wilber for this clarification.)

So, a religious leader, for example, may have high spiritual develoment, average interpersonal development, and low moral development. Therefore, he may be a charismatic leader, a mediocre church manager, and a poor risk at a moment that requires him to choose right action. At that time, despite his other gifts, he may be unable to stop his shadow from acting out.

In the same way, a believer may be highly developed cognitively, thinking through religious teachings, but poorly developed emotionally, leaving her vulnerable to denial or to silence at a charged moment. As potential abuse approaches, she may not be able to identify how she feels, to know why she feels that way, or to articulate it for self-defense.

Meeting the shadow of addiction

For some Westerners, the unsurpassed rise of science and technology has meant a rejection of religious life. However, the holy longing stirs in us—and only spirit can properly contain it. If a religious or spiritual context is not available to channel our yearning, it will find other objects of desire. And the more concrete and mundane realms of life will be forced to carry it: our lovers, our work, and our food, drugs, and alcohol.

Before Bill W. launched Alcoholics Anonymous, Jung told him that the craving for alcohol was equivalent, on a low level, to the spiritual thirst for union with god. This profound insight may have led the founders of AA to build their organization on a spiritual foundation.

It also helped me to realize that any addiction—alcohol, drugs, food, sex, gambling, shopping—masks our holy longing. A chocolate cookie, a Vodka, a hit of ecstasy, a roll of the dice, a designer dress—each can carry the projection of the Self or *imago dei*. Each can hold out the promise of a high that alters our state of consciousness one last time. And the craving for each of these objects of desire hides our deeper craving for transcendence. These substitute highs camouflage our holy longing with a temporary solution, a quick fix, which only leaves us hungering for more.

So, the battle is joined: to drink or not to drink, to eat or not to eat. The forbidden object becomes dangerous and revered.

In *The Thirst for Wholeness,* Christina Grof described her feeling of holy longing since childhood: "The pit of my stomach felt empty, my heart hurt, and my entire being aspired toward something I could not identify. As I grew, the ache in my soul permeated all aspects of my life. I felt monumentally homesick for something undefined, for an unnamed entity, place, or experience. Nothing I did alleviated the yearning within me."

Then she found the delicious oblivion of alcohol. "My boundaries melted, the pain disappeared, and I was free. I felt comfortable in my own skin. I was at ease with people, included, accepted, cherished—until alcohol turned against me."

In a frantic effort to fill the void, many people consume enormous amounts of alcohol, cigarettes, and drugs. Trying to beat their addictions, they feel intense relief and remorse in the first stages of withdrawal. But for most addicts, a repetitive cycle occurs: intense craving, obsessive thoughts about the forbidden, desired object, then a burst of acting out, which is often accompanied by euphoria. Addicts will then try to push their longing away or, alternately, find another way to gratify it. But, ultimately, neither denial of the craving nor compromise with it will work.

Marion Woodman wrote of this phenomenon in the context of eating disorders in *Addiction to Perfection*. Obese and anorexic women battle for consciousness through their acceptance or rejection of food, she said. They project the *imago* onto the forbidden food and want to eat it, to commune with that which they have projected outward. People who binge will eat until the ego gives up and surrenders to a larger, archetypal force.

On the other hand, people who starve themselves will fast or exercise until they feel light and weightless. They want to leave the mire of matter, Woodman said, to fly with the spirit.

In either case, Woodman suggested that these compulsions replace meaningful rituals that previously offered religious transcendence. In submitting to a spiritual rite, we invoke the gods, offer up the ego for sacrifice, and feel reborn in a new level of awareness. But alcohol does not replace spirit, and starving does not replace fasting. In each case, the concrete is substituted for the symbolic. And voluntary submission of the ego to a greater force is replaced by involuntary, repetitive routine.

Those who successfully and finally eliminate a craving for a substance discover that, beneath it, a deeper craving remains. Buddhism teaches that all emotional stress comes about because of craving or *tanha,* which translates as thirst. This addictive yearning, which cannot be filled, is not fundamentally different from other cravings. But it reminds me of the Buddhist teaching about hungry ghosts, creatures who have swollen bellies but needle-thin necks. Even though they are surrounded by food, they cannot satisfy their hunger or thirst because they can eat or drink only one drop at a time.

In her book *Holy Hunger*, Margaret Bullitt-Jonas described her struggle with binge eating as rooted in warring desires. She wanted to make a speech that her unavailable father would listen to in silence. And she didn't want to utter a word; she was defeated before she began. She wanted to weep in her sad mother's arms and hear that her feelings were okay. And she wanted to run from such intimacy and self-exposure. She wanted to live inside every inch of her body and be at home inside her skin. And she wanted to be rid of her body and punish it for its needs. She wanted her life to be unpredictable and fresh. And she wanted to be in complete control. She wanted to be awake, vital, and alive. And she wanted to be asleep, entirely numb.

Finally, she said, she had no idea what she most deeply desired. And she played out her dilemma with food. One day she could trust the desire to be open to life and eat lightly. The next day she would be gripped by the need to control and binge. Her mind became a tyrant, her body its prisoner. She became a woman who was perpetually restless, afraid of her inner emptiness, unable to listen to her longing. Instead, her longing spun out into insatiable craving. She choked off words and filled up the silence with food.

Through Overeaters Anonymous, prayer, and telling her true story, Bullitt-Jones eventually discovered that it was not food she desired after all. When she stopped attaching her desires to food, a larger, deeper desire could flow through her, a desire for something infinite, something elusive yet present. She called it a power that welcomes her passions and her hunger, a power that does not eliminate desires, but transforms them.

When we meet the spiritual Other in addiction, we no longer consciously inhabit our holy longing. We become its captive. And we are pulled beneath the waves of desire, even to the point of drowning. But if we can redirect our longing toward the holy, the undertow can deliver us to the next level of awareness. And in this way addiction becomes a vehicle of evolution.

Death and transcendence

A few years ago I was saddened and disturbed by the death of Nigel Watts, author of *The Way of Love,* a short tale about the life of Sufi poet Jelaluddin Rumi. Watts reported that he planned to commit suicide because he could no longer bear separation from the beloved, the Sufi name for god. And so he did.

His story reminded me of the members of Heaven's Gate, a small cult that committed mass suicide in 1997 because they believed that, with the passing of a comet, they would be taken by a UFO to another level of life. As one member put it, "I look forward to our next major step, shedding these creatures [the human body] and moving on to the next evolutionary level."

More recently, as of this writing, we are faced with the enigma of suicide bombers who attacked the Twin Towers in New York and continue to attack civilian sites in Israel, blowing themselves up in the process. Why did all of these people devoutly desire death, even long for it?

As more information has emerged about the terrorists, we in the West have been even more surprised. In an article on the topic, psychoanalyst Joan Lachkar reported in "The California Therapist" (March/April 2002) that support and encouragement for suicidal killings runs deep through Muslim culture. Young children try on the clothing of suicide bombers. Pictures of those who died in this manner adorn walls and books. Teachers praise martyrs, and a popular film portrays a young Egyptian boy who blows up Israeli soldiers and himself as a hero, while the audience cheers.

Lachlar described suicide bombers as traumatized children who were emotionally abandoned, suffered severe loss and betrayal, and were raised by unavailable or violent caretakers. The result: due to their rage and shame and their inability or lack of opportunity to heal, they are overcome with a desire to retaliate.

Enter their hero, Osama bin Laden, who provides them with an enemy to hate and an ideology to relieve their uncertainty and to back up their dissonant feelings. Their fragmented sense of self merges with him, their ideal *imago*, and takes on the group identity. Their sense of powerlessness dissolves; their lack of meaning and purpose dissipates. They are willing to die for the cause—even eager to die, because in death they will meet Allah and his prophet, the objects of their longing.

I would add that beyond or beneath the personal histories of those who yearn for death lie religious tenets that support that inclination. Believers who become identified with the "up" arc, the Self or spirit, tend to devalue life in the body, its creature comforts and sufferings. I suggest that their unconscious depression or psychic numbness colludes with these teachings, which devalue matter as "earthly fetters" and, therefore, they long for the other world.

Split off from modes of transcendence *in* life, they come to mistake death for transcendence—death as a path to god. They yearn for physical death because symbolic death is unavailable or unknown.

In the end, few faithful believers can live indefinitely cut off from their own emotional vitality and intuitive wisdom. Eventually, they will want to reclaim their emotional shadows. Few can live indefinitely in a passive, dependent, child-like state. Eventually, they will feel their powerlessness mount and will want to reclaim their autonomy. Few can live indefinitely while projecting their *imago dei* onto a limited, mortal human being. Eventually, they will meet the spiritual shadow and suffer feelings of disillusionment and loss of faith.

At the same time, few religious leaders can carry the burden of this projection indefinitely. Jung asserted that possession by an archetype turns a person into a flat, collective figure, a mask behind which he can no longer develop as an individual. Eventually, because he carries only the light and colludes in ignoring his own dark side, it may act out impulsively in hypocritical or even abusive behavior. It may act out in coercing others to die.

Following the revelation about her Zen teacher's affairs, Katy Butler wrote, "My black meditation robe still hangs in the back of closet. I never lost faith in

Buddhist teachings, but for some years I didn't know how to reconnect with them. Instead, I did what a friend called remedial work, examining my personal history and the anger and self-righteousness I experienced when the scandal broke. I was among those who hoped to find a sanctuary within Buddhism for my personal wounds. But my culture and family history trailed me into my community like a can tied to the tail of a dog."

For me, remedial work involved turning from the light to the dark side, from the Via Positiva to the Via Negativa, or shifting my psychic energy and attention from spirit to shadow. During that transition, I wrote the following piece.

Midlogue: My Longing for the Dark: A Meditation on Down

My father dreamed of becoming an astronaut, shooting up and away from our blue pearl, up until he would step out, in rarified air, onto a red world with no downward pull.

I dreamed of becoming a yogi, shooting up and away from my mortal coil, up until I would step out, in rarified air, onto a golden world with no downward pull.

Like him, I dreamed of up, while everything around me moved inexorably down, down into decay, down into dirt. Today I turn my ear toward the quiet call of the dirt. I turn my ear toward the whisper beneath the dirt, the whisper beckoning me down, down to the land of Down.

It is a large turning—from up to down. It is a change of direction as pivotal as reorienting the compass needle from North to South. It is as if my compass had been leading me away from myself, up and away from my bodily juices, up and away from my cravings for sweets, up and away from my earthly diggings for grasses and tubers and blooms.

And now the return has begun. The silver ship is plunging down from heights into depths, down from light into dark, down from heaven into hell. What is this linguistic force that, like gravity, pulls certain words together, creating allies, and separates others, creating walls? Why do down/deep/dark/dirty seem wed together with the familiarity of ageless mates? And why do they seem to be fit bedfellows for the making of soul? On the other hand, why do up/high/light/pure seem like the recipe ingredients for a life of spirit?

Is the dream of up a defense against down? Must the longing for spiritual ascent be a denial of soulful descent?

For me, down and up seem separated by an endless winding wall, forever sundered into the realms of hell and heaven, each with its own gods, each with its own demons.

I grew up with the gods of Up, looking down on me and wagging their fingers of scorn. But who are the gods of Down?

The dark stranger who leaps out of a crack in the earth is Hades, lord of the underworld, also known as Pluto. He enters Greek mythology as a son of Cronos, brother to Hestia, Demeter, Hera, Poseidon, and Zeus. Cronos, according to myth, swallowed his children because he feared they would overpower him. So, according to one legend, Hades remained in his father's womb for many years.

But, according to another legend, Hades was thrown, as an infant, into the far reaches of the underworld, and there he remained in darkness forever.

The myth "Hymn to Demeter," the only story to include Hades, introduces him as he abducts the innocent maiden Persephone, who is gathering flowers, and carries her off to his dark home. Most of the interpretations of the Eleusinian mysteries focus on the nature of Demeter, the quintessential mother and goddess of grain, and Persephone, the mother-bound virgin who becomes queen of the underworld. But who is Hades, this god of Down? What is it about him that makes us fear his realm? Is Hades a violent rapist or he is a sexual initiator for the maiden? Does he help her to break the overly close bond with her mother and thus find her womanhood? Or does he violate their intimacy with a force that is unforgiving? Certainly, he carries her over the wall that divides up from down; he guides her from the light world of ego into the dark world of soul.

This god of Down has several names: Trophonios means the nourisher; Polydegmon means the receiver of many guests; Euboulos means the good counselor; Ploutos means the wealthgiver; Zeus Chthonios means the underworld side of the all-seeing god of Olympus. And, finally, Aldoneus means the unseen one, the invisible god. Thus Hades has many aspects that are associated with fertility, generosity, even wisdom. But, ultimately, he remains hidden, lord of a separate realm, not lord among people or houses or trees.

Even the everyday vernacular reveals biases against the realm of Hades, prejudices that are deeply built into our ways of seeing and feeling: When we have the blues, we say, "I am feeling down." So down means unhappy, dejected, downhearted.

When we dislike something, one says, "I'm down on it."

When we have a bad habit, we say, "It's my downfall."

When people are "down" on their luck, they are known as "downtrodden."

Even those who live uptown are seen as more fortunate than those who live downtown.

So, down and up are habits of mind which, like all habits, cause the seeing to be blind. For if we view down as a falling to be avoided, and if we view up as a rising to be strived for, then we cannot see the gifts of every small downward move. And we cannot feel movement unless it is felt as forward and up.

Down is more than a figure of speech: it holds a whole archetypal world, a realm that has come to be associated in depth psychology with a movement toward soul, an orientation toward feeling, toward body, toward the unconscious psyche. One does therapy to uncover depths in the self, to go down into the pain, down into the psyche, the promised land.

A few years ago I noticed that I had silently, unknowingly begun to associate going down, feeling deeply, with feeling sad. I had associated down with an emotional state, or array of states, limited to sadness—sorrow, melancholy, depression, grief. This, I had come to feel, was the only appropriate response to the state of human suffering when it is viewed honestly, that is, with depth. So people who seemed happy, complacent, upbeat, and optimistic also seemed shallow, to have no depth and no appropriateness in their response to human suffering.

In other words, *up,* which had carried light in the first half of my life, began to carry shadow. And *down,* which had been disowned, began to carry light.

If the larger world, the Judeo-Christian framework, favors up, the move away from the Fall and toward the Resurrection, then the alternative world, the framework of critique, which questions cultural assumptions, might naturally favor down. This compensatory move helps us stay conscious—until we fall, once again, into unquestioning gravitational fields of words.

I notice my use of "falling" here, and it makes me wonder why we can't fall up. I realize it just may be our gravitational world that divides the pie of reality into up and down, generating the fantasy of flight as freedom from gravitation and the fantasy of ascent as liberation from suffering.

For me, certainly, Hades was an abductor; he stole me away from the upper world where I was gathering flowers of innocence. He pierced my spiritual persona and forced me to face all that I had sought to avoid, all that I had hoped to escape by dedication to the light. And he initiated me in the darkness of my own cave, where I left dreams and ideals, family and friends far behind.

Like Persephone, who becomes the bride of Hades and resides with him in darkness for half the year, then returns to her mother in the upper world during the other half, I, too, can now hold the darkness and the light. When I arise from the underworld, I carry its darkness with me now; I carry its stillness and loss. And if I move too far up and begin to float away, I can hear Hades whisper beneath the dirt, beckoning me down, down to the fertile land of Down.

From suffering I have learned this: that whoever is sore wounded by love will never be made whole unless she embrace the very same love that wounded her.

—Mechtilde of Magdeburg

What we have to be is what we are.

—Thomas Merton

When Zusya, a Hasidic rabbi, was criticized for unorthodox behavior, he replied, 'In the next world I will not be asked why in this life I was not Moses, but rather why I was not Zusya.'

—A Hasidic tale

I do not seek to follow in the footsteps of the men of old; I seek the things they sought.

—Basho

6

Rekindling the Flame: Shadow-work for Spiritual Abuse and Disillusionment

A fortunate few find the narrow path through the darkness and undergo an authentic intitation: we travel from spiritual innocence through the dark descent toward a new level of consciousness—spiritual maturity. We evolve from dependency on a spiritual parent through meeting the shadow toward spiritual adulthood.

Having been emptied out of old ideas and images, having been left fallow for a dark season, we become fertile soil for new life—open but not naïve, eager but not impatient, and ripe for blossoming.

With practice, we learn to meet the darkness in ourselves and in our priests or teachers, gradually coming to accept it as a part of being human. No longer susceptible to being true believers and perpetrating fundamentalism, we may be able to see our own shadows, accept the limitations of our teachers, and empathize more deeply with others who hold diverse views.

We learn to trace some of the roots of our religious longings to early family issues (feelings of isolation, emptiness, or low self-worth, patterns of victimization and caretaking, a need to feel special, an inability to face limits, an inability to deal with negative emotions or conflict, and a driving perfectionism). And we learn to acknowledge the dark sides of our spiritual beliefs, working through overly simplistic, black-and-white ideas, until we can eventually hold greater paradox and ambiguity.

For some, this inner work requires separation from an esteemed teacher, which can evoke powerful feelings of loss, guilt, anxiety, and shame. It may require separation from an institutionalized community or an informal group, which also leads to intense feelings of isolation and loss. And it may require separation from a set of teachings or a philosophy, which triggers strong feelings of meaningless and purposelessness.

I don't offer a universal prescription here, suggesting that readers reject a church or tradition. Instead, I suggest that we work toward making conscious "the religious unconscious." That is, we begin to contemplate the underside of our spiritual lives, questioning the dubious behaviors of our priests or teachers, as well as the authoritative assumptions we have taken for granted. In this way, we can begin to see through those beliefs that maintain our suffering and our shame. We can begin to see through those *imagoes* that block our transcendence.

In the end, shadow-work for spiritual abuse and disillusionment requires that we reclaim lost parts of the self—self-worth, independent thinking, emotional shadows, bodily awareness, the capacity to initiate action, and images of god—that did not fit our spiritual persona. Or permit entirely new feelings and images to emerge. And it requires that we reclaim those parts—power, wisdom, compassion—that were sacrificed in a projection onto an idealized teacher because our capacity to carry our own greatness was so diminished.

Communal shadow-work

In a *Common Boundary* article (May 1990), Katy Butler described a ceremony used by Buddhist monks in the first few centuries after the Buddha's death. On the eve of every full and new moon, they gathered in the forest for "confession before the community." There they publicly recited the Buddhist precepts, admitted their shortcomings, their violations, and any damage they had done to their community.

Butler suggested that if we reinstated such a quiet ritual, a brave, disgraced teacher or priest might safely acknowledge his or her misconduct. He might disclose the wounds that brought him to perpetrate it. Perhaps the *sangha* or congregation could confess its deep disappointment and feelings of betrayal. Its members could acknowledge their participation in denial and rationalization. And the whole group could apologize to those members who had been mistreated and compensate them in some way. After full acknowledgment and restitution, healing might be possible.

In a few cases, communities have attempted to make amends in this way. Some individual members of the clergy who perpetrated abuse and received treatment have acknowledged the harmful effects of their behavior and attempted to make restitution. For example, Episcopal priest Father Leo Booth wrote openly in his books about his own recovery from alcoholism and religious addiction, which he defined as using god, a church, or a belief system to escape reality and elevate self-worth. However, Booth insisted that individual treament is not enough. He urged both clergy and parishioners to examine how the church perpetuates destructive, shaming beliefs and enables religious abuse.

He pointed out that many church-goers are raised to have a childlike fear of displeasing god, which leaves them vulnerable to exploitation. In the church's sexist, patriarchal system, he said, god is father, Christ is son, and women are left out. The resulting imbalance of power is reinforced by liturgy and doctrine. Covert messages—"God is the judge who punishes or rewards us"; "God will provide if we obey"; "If we truly trust in Him, we won't have doubts"; "Clergy have power over us because they are superior"; "God wants selflessness, self-love is a sin"—lead us to abandon large parts of ourselves.

These kinds of destructive messages are not the sole province of the church. They can be heard in most traditions that are patriarchal, controlling, shaming, or based on abuse of power. I recall one meditation teacher telling me that his form of practice was the only way to enlightenment; others were a waste of time. Another told group members that if they did not meditate enough, they would be responsible for the lack of peace in the world.

To prevent religious abuse, Booth said, we must be willing to revise the institutional elements that create and maintain it. In other words, community-wide repair needs to include education, support, and methods of restitution for victims, perpetrators, and other members. Some experts have suggested that priests, rabbis, and *roshis* follow the same code of ethics as doctors and therapists. That is, inappropriate contact between a leader and a member of the flock is a breach of professional boundaries. Others argue that legally institutionalizing boundaries has not helped therapists to stop violating them. Rather, thorough and ongoing education about projection, transference, and boundaries might go further to help professionals internalize boundaries and protect those under their care.

Today Father Booth's words seem prescient: following the many accusations of sexual abuse by priests, both believers and experts alike are calling for institutional reform in the church. Because huge, wealthy institutions are by nature conservative, built to support the status quo, such reform is unlikely. However, the church's central metaphor might help at this time: the institution itself is undergoing a crucifixion and descent. If it is allowed to die as it is, like the dying and resurrecting Christ, it may be able to be reborn to a new life.

In addition, I suggest that individual religious and spiritual teachers must learn to recognize and manage their own shadow material. If they knew their own areas of vulnerability, the ways in which they might act out under pressure, they could anticipate them, find other outlets, or even ask for support. Finally, spiritual guides need to practice self-care in such a way that they are not socially or professionally isolated and, therefore, likely to fall into inflation or self-deception.

At the California Psychological Convention in March 1998, Nanette de Fuentes suggested several stages of congregational healing from clergy abuse: 1) shock ("I can't believe this"); 2) denial ("I won't believe this"); 3) bargaining ("What if he stayed part time?"); 4) anger ("Is she making up the charges?"); 5) depression ("Will anyone come here again?"); 6) holy rage ("How can we cleanse the priesthood?"); 7) and, finally, acceptance.

However, she agreed with Booth that while individuals go through these successive stages, there can be no real healing without justice-making. That is, the truth must be told. The abuser must be named and condemned. The victim must be heard and protected from further abuse. The abuser must face consequences and make tangible restitution.

A handful of spiritual teachers have publicly admitted their wrongdoing and worked toward reclaiming those parts of themselves that were sacrificed by carrying the ideal *imago* for others. Their openness and authenticity may one day lead the way for other teachers and clergy to come forward and acknowledge their own grandiosity and their own limitations. If so, we could re-imagine religious institutions in a climate of greater openness. We could re-imagine the priest/parishioner or teacher/student relationship in a climate of greater trust because this openness and trust would be built on hard-won awareness and a concern for the well-being of others, rather than on a fear of external authority and punishment.

For example, according to *Yoga Journal* (Nov. 1994), Yogi Amrit Desai, an adept in kundalini practice and founder of the Kripalu yoga ashram in Massachusetts, taught that sex would slow students' progress toward enlightenment and that celibacy would enhance kundalini or spiritual energy. In 1994, when a woman disciple told others that she had sexual relations with Desai because he told her that it was a spiritual gift and special privilege, he denied her story. And his denial was accepted by the community, even by the woman's husband and son, who remained at the ashram after she left.

Another woman came forward with the same claim. This time, Desai admitted both affairs and confirmed a third. He resigned and offered to pay for the womens' therapy. He also made a public apology to the community.

His students were outraged, heartbroken, and deeply demoralized. The man who carried their *imago dei* had habitually violated the moral code he imposed on them. Long-buried resentments surfaced. As one disciple told *Yoga Journal*, "I feel murderous rage at having sold out my voice to the guru. People here are under a great hypnosis. We don't see ourselves because the focus is on an exotic spokesperson of the truth who embodies beauty, grace, and the power of the lineage. Try standing next to someone of that stature and that degree of realization and finding your voice."

To facilitate the healing process, Kripalu staff invited a diverse group of psychotherapists to assist them in dealing with unresolved emotional and interpersonal issues that years of yoga practice left untouched. The radical result: at Kripalu, the traditional guru/disciple relationship has been recast in a more egalitarian mold. Those who used to adore their teacher uncritically no longer blindly accept his infallibility. In fact, teacher and students are learning together and from their more reciprocal relationship.

As Desai told his students, "If you have a conflict with me and I don't live it fully—if I blame you or feel ashamed—then that experience goes under the carpet, into the dark area. It just waits there until somebody else pushes the button. Then the same fear that I had in my dealings with you comes back. The seed didn't burn to ashes. That's why my determination in this lifetime is to face everything."

Since his resignation, a council of long-term residents is helping to shape community policy and form a new vision that takes the focus off the guru. The nature of service at the ashram has changed as well: students no longer work around the clock for a dollar each month. They now put in forty hours each week and receive stipends and insurance. Although celibacy is required for single residents, marriage is permitted.

Desai told *Yoga Journal*: "Many students who came to Kripalu experienced the feeling of finally coming home and the possibility of living in a conscious community with a guru, a spiritual father who would nurture their spirits, love and care for them. But in order to keep the dream alive, they suppressed a lot of their feelings. In time, these were destined to shatter the dreams. We tend to believe that love ends when dreams are demolished. In reality, the shattering of dreams is the opportunity for the emergence of true love."

In the beginning, Desai thought his role was fixing and teaching. But the traditional model from India was not addressing the issues of his students around childhood abuse, parental authority, and self-expression. He now says he understands that, as old childhood wounds surfaced, people needed him to recognize and feel their pain and hurt, not give spiritual answers.

In some ways, he said, the teaching of the guru-disciple relationship of love, selfless service, and surrender reinforced codependence and suppression. Residents transferred their feelings about parental authority to him. "I and those at Kripalu are determined to use the failure of the dream as an opportunity to enter into an authentic relationship. The new level of honesty is sometimes uncomfortable for us.

"We are dismantling the old form. It calls for a profound shift in my role. I am using this shift to let go of my attachment to the parental role, my self-concept, my ego. I'm now exploring how to blend yoga with western psychotherapy to create a new model. There is no map. Life is demanding that I challenge many assumptions about the guru/disciple relationship that I used to hold as true, so that something new can be born."

In *Avalanche*, physician-turned-healer Brugh Joy also openly explored his own fall from grace. In his early life, Brugh deeply identified with the Self in the *imago* of Christ—inspired savior, teacher, redeemer. Therefore, he longed for the light, experienced altered states, developed healing abilities, overvalued spirituality—and split off the shadow sides of his nature.

But, thirty years later, the shadow erupted in a dream: seated in a car, he looked into the rearview mirror and locked eyes with "evil incarnate." Attending to the message from his unconscious, Brugh allowed this dream to penetrate him and change him. The result: the encounter "raped his innocence," as he put it, and initiated him into his own vulnerability, which had been disowned.

This shift appeared in his life in many ways. For example, as a teacher at the Findhorn community in Scotland, Brugh had been loved and appreciated, even venerated, carrying an ideal *imago*. But on a later visit, he spoke to the community about the negative consequences of feeling special and the risks of identifying with light over darkness. Following these remarks, he was attacked by his listeners because his statements were heretical in the new age community. And he suddenly became the object of a negative projection, a scapegoat.

Brugh realized that the shadow of the community was erupting—and he was the mirror. He also recognized that those qualities that were attacked were parts of himself, not merely disowned parts of his attacker. He was able to view the event as an initiation into carrying a collective shadow projection, just as politicians do.

Finally, Brugh could see that spiritual viewpoints are filters that accept and reject certain feelings, thoughts, and images. As such, they exclude whole chunks of life, including aspects of the divine itself. "If you can't give up the power that is yours through identification with the deity that is dancing you—warrior, saint, healer, mother, father—you are seduced and in danger of losing your soul."

In an effort to transcend to the next level of consciousness, he wrote, we need to surrender our attachment to the power of the archetype that is dominant. And the consequences of that act may include humiliation, powerlessness, and a loss of sacred values. But it also may mean our evolution.

Separating from a teacher and *imago dei*

When the disciple is ready, the guru disappears.

—Gregory Bogart

When we have to imagine an object of attraction as evil, dark, and demonic, we do so to be able to have some control over it, to help us break the power of its attraction.

—Brugh Joy

For students, the required sacrifice may mean letting go of identification with being a student and moving out of a naïve, childlike role. As long as we remain in an obedient, dependent position, we banish many of our own qualities into the shadow, including our inquisitiveness, financial ambitions, sexual needs, and creative longings. In this way, our own development is derailed.

Research on people in religious communities has confirmed this finding: despite radical ideological changes and initial relief from inner conflicts, many members' basic traits and unconscious conflicts remain intractable or reappear with their departure from the fold. One client continued to see herself as an outsider even while she fully participated within the group for many years. A middle-aged man continued to act rebellious in his church congregation, as he had in his family. And a young woman kept trying to live up to the perfectionism of her demanding father with her spiritual father.

In each case, the recreation of parent-child or family dynamics in a religious community may not lead to their resolution. Instead, these people need to separate from their surrogate parents and families in order to step into a more independent, responsible, adult position so that their internal development can continue.

Some students may be able to accomplish this task by remaining with the community as a loyally dissenting member. Others may see through their projections, move to the margins of the community, and even continue their practices. But some will need to break their ties, separating altogether from the priest or teacher and the group.

When the student is faced with an inner conflict between her devotion and her growing individuality, difficult challenges typically arise. If she has been encouraged to meditate on the teacher or merge with him in a symbiotic way, she may have difficulty finding her own separate boundaries. If she has projected an *imago dei* and has an idealizing transference, she may, through gradual disappointments, see the human being more clearly behind the ideal image. This recognition may enable her to leave with tender feelings. Or she may be devastated by the appearance of the teacher's shadow, unable to maintain her own self-worth without allying with his perfection, and begin the search for a new, more perfect ideal.

If the aspirant has enjoyed service to the teacher or to the church, she may feel that without that outlet she has no direction or purpose. If she has learned to distrust her own impulses, she may wonder if her need to separate stems from her own selfishness or laziness. Typically, these self-doubts will be fueled by negative messages from the group, which may criticize her doubts and discourage her efforts toward independence.

If she has buried feelings of inferiority, envy, or resentment beneath her admiration, they may rush to the surface, leaving her with deep ambivalence toward her teacher. This process is evident in the history of psychoanalysis, in which each of Freud's disciples struggled with the guilt of differentiating from him and the fear of his rejection. In the end, most ended up by turning the "good father" into the "bad father," or symbolically killing him off, in order to do their own creative work. A few, instead, killed themselves.

Ira Progroff called this conflict "the disciple's dilemma." It's a tension between feeling dependent, grateful, and fulfilled as a student and feeling the need for more autonomy, self-expression, and fulfillment from other sources. In many cases, this tension forces the student's separation.

For all of these reasons, the onset of this passage is filled with confusion, fear, guilt, and loss. As former Zen priest Josh Baran put it when he left his community, "The leaving process was the most difficult transition of my life. And during this period I gained more insight than in the previous ten years."

Some believers can be aided during this time by images that arise spontaneously in dreams and creative works. Gregory Bogart reported several clients' dreams as they worked through the process of separation from spiritual teachers (*Journal of Transpersonal Psychology*, 1992, vol. 24, no. 1). One man, who spent years in an ashram with vows of celibacy and poverty, struggled with a desire to leave and marry. He dreamed that he entered a large meditation hall in which hundreds of seats were arranged facing away from the guru's seat up front.

According to Bogart, the dream portrayed his readiness to remain in a reverential relationship with the teacher but with his attention directed away from the guru and toward the world.

Another man, who suffered from a series of painful disillusionments with several teachers, worked deeply to release his negative feelings toward them. He dreamed that he was in a lush green meadow, standing near a large, very ancient and beautiful tree. He was observing a vigil for his dead teacher and father, who was buried beneath the tree. It was a solemn moment, yet he was at peace.

Bogart's client felt that the burial of his dead teacher and father signified the death of his need for an external spiritual guide and heralded the emergence of his capacity to become his own source of wisdom. As the client said, "Now, with these men fertilizing my roots, I can become my own father."

Finally, I cannot fail to mention another reason for leaving a spiritual guide: aside from completion of a psychological journey, in which developmental needs demand more autonomy, a student's spiritual journey may demand it. After all, we submit to a teacher with the promise of a new level of consciousness and, for a few, this does occur. Once we realize our own divine nature and internalize the *imago dei,* the teacher's purpose has been fulfilled.

Reclaiming the light

As Nelson Mandela said in his 1994 inaugural speech as president of South Africa, "Our deepest fear is not that we are inadequate, our deepest fear is that we are powerful beyond measure. It is our light, not our darkness, that most frightens us."

Perhaps that is why, when we find a beloved priest or teacher, we so easily give away our light, our spiritual authority, and permit another to carry our flame. We come to believe that he or she alone can mediate the divine for us. We are not made in god's image; the one who carries our *imago dei* alone is. So, we are no longer burdened with a direct relationship to our own light, our own radiance, our own Self.

As a result, we identify with a narrow range of archetypes: the student, the seeker, the believer, the child. If we become an obedient spiritual son or daughter to a surrogate parent, we cut off those qualities that adhere to the adult self. If we disown all of the light, we carry those qualities that we attribute to the darkness, such as evil sinner, doubting Thomas, or lazy meditator. If we are spiritually abused, we may become identified with being a victim, which leaves us guilty, ashamed, and disempowered.

In the end, during the separation from the teacher or teachings, spiritual shadow-work requires us to retrieve those qualities that we attributed to the teacher or priest. When we have internalized them and brought them back into our own treasury, we will carry our own light. And we will be able to live out a wider range of archetypes, providing a richer, deeper life.

In *The Direct Path*, Andrew Harvey described his own difficult journey of reclaiming the light from Indian teacher Mother Meera. As a devotee, Harvey was instructed by Meera to get married and write a book claiming that her divine force had changed him from gay to heterosexual. As a result of that painful encounter, in which she asked her devotee to tell a lie, Harvey saw through the projections that led him to exalt her as "divine mother." Angry and disappointed, he faced the dark shadow of his teacher and made a painful, difficult decision.

He went public with her request and his objection. In response, Meera denied having made it. As a result of the controversy, he lost a teaching job, became ill, and received threats against his life. During a fierce attempt at self-reflection, he stripped down his beliefs to their essentials and allowed himself to undergo a rite of passage.

Five years later, divested of trust in the traditional teacher/student system, he wrote the book that is about communion with god without a human mediator. "Without this radical disillusionment," he wrote, "I would have continued to project, in more and more subtle ways, my own divine truth and essence onto Meera or Rumi or the Dalai Lama, and so would have avoided the ultimate adventure—to claim complete responsibility, in and under god, for one's own spiritual development."

If Harvey had continued to believe that his development was an effect of the guru's grace, he said, he would never have claimed the depths of his own realization or known that he would make deeper and more honest spiritual progress outside the guru system which, at that stage, kept him diminished.

Reclaiming independent thinking

Although we may need outer authority for guidance at some stages of life, at another we need to develop beyond these parental figures and cultivate our internal resources—our own ideas, beliefs, feelings, intuitions, images, and actions.

In his book *The Double Mirror*, Tibetan Buddhist student Stephen Butterfield described the process of relinquishing his doubts and queries in order to follow a Buddhist path. He had a lot of questions for his teacher, Trungpa Rinpoche. But the teacher responded, "Do not intellectualize overmuch. Just do the practices, and their cumulative wisdom will be come apparent as you go along."

Butterfield tried to follow this advice, but he was never able to completely silence his questions or find satisfactory answers to them. Instead, his questions went underground, banished into the shadow, so that he could gain Trungpa's acceptance, belong in the *sangha*, and receive initiations.

After a long series of disappointments and betrayals, Butterfield could no longer stand the tension between the sustenance of his inner experience and the destructiveness of his organization and its teachers. So, he stopped practicing.

And all his questions erupted—those he had ignored because they were too threatening and those he had carefully avoided because he believed they would block his way. Some questions were too basic to ask without embarrassment. Others revealed pride and egotism or resistance to the guru, which was fatal.

Why was he doing the practices? What did they have to do with enlightenment? Is Buddhism a vehicle or a crutch or a shell, useful only until we hatch from it? Does Buddhism even exist apart from the activity of minds using it as a frame of reference? And were the robed men to whom he had bowed over and over any more awake than anyone else? And if they were not, who was? And, finally, if his questions were coming back as a result of not practicing, then was his practice repressing them?

This loss of independent thinking may occur within any tradition. A former member of Herbert W. Armstrong's Worldwide Church of God told me that, when the "prophet's" end-of-the-world predictions failed to come true, he was terrified of questioning their validity. He still held out the hope that, at Armageddon, he would be saved with the rest of the faithful. So, he submerged his doubts.

But, years later, when allegations of incest surfaced about Armstrong, my client's doubts forcefully erupted into consciousness: perhaps Armstrong was not all-perfect or all-knowing. Perhaps he was flawed. Or human. The seismic force of those thoughts shook his belief system and broke him open. Slowly, and with support, he worked to develop a more complex and nuanced view of his religious teacher. He became able to value certain qualities in Armstrong and to reject others, to appreciate certain teachings and to disclaim others for himself.

A similar process occurred for a client who was raised in the Christian Science church. When her elderly parents, who were life-long members, became gravely ill and had to choose between using medicine or facing death, they both went to a doctor for the first time in their lives. As a result, their church shunned them. My client reported, "It was horrible to watch these two old people being abandoned by the very church they had supported. I had seen miraculous healings and had felt the sweetness of community. But with this act of judgment and rejection of my parents, all of my doubts came crashing in."

Our religious leaders and institutions teach us that we must choose between faith and doubt. So, to be believers, we bury our doubts and adopt the languages and beliefs of our communities. Our longing for certainty and our intolerance of ambiguity lead us to seek simple, black and white answers.

As a result, we give the power of definition over our lives to others. They circumscribe how we spend our time and money, how we eat, dress, have sex, marry—and what we believe. They delimit right thinking and behavior from wrong. They define who is on god's side and who is not. They proclaim who is going to heaven or becoming enlightened and who is not. As believers, we gain certainty, access to the sacred, and the promise of salvation. Therefore, our questions become taboo, forbidden thoughts that threaten to topple the system of beliefs.

Instead, I suggest that we cultivate the faith to doubt—the trust or confidence to explore more fully and honestly what we actually believe. And our forbidden thoughts can show the way: they can guide us toward the shadow where, like hidden treasure, our disowned ideas, opinions, and doubts lie dormant.

When I was beginning to separate from my meditation community, I remember thinking that there must be some value to emotional attachment, which in my tradition was viewed as a trap in *samsara*, the transitory world of suffering. Until that thought snuck up on me, I deeply believed that the only way to liberation was to remain free of all attachment, whether to comfort, love, money, beauty, or another human being.

But that forbidden thought opened a tightly shut door: I could see that my attachment to non-attachment had deeply personal, emotional roots. That spiritual premise supported my terrors of intimacy, sexuality, failure, and death. I gradually came to believe that I needed to face those fears by going through them, rather than avoiding them. I needed to take a psychological journey through my fears before I reached a level of consciousness in which non-attachment might emerge spontaneously.

This led me to sort out other teachings that I had absorbed without discrimination. For example, before becoming a meditation teacher I had been a political activist. But when I came to believe that meditation reached the source of problems—consciousness—and, therefore, it was pointless to struggle with symptoms, I stopped all political and social action. Today I see the narrowness of this assumption: a spiritual practice that is purely introverted and without any social engagement risks self-absorption. It also risks colluding with oppressive and corrupt political and economic systems and, therefore, furthering the suffering of other human beings.

I came to conclude that, while my practice held great value in the spiritual line of development, it had severe limits. And some of the teachings surrounding it were inadequate or even destructive. This distinction enabled me to reclaim my independent thinking and my faith to doubt. I could affirm my holy longing, while clarifying the extent to which my attitude toward meditation had hampered my emotional, cognitive, and political development.

Finally, I could begin to hold both the positive and negative sides of my experience, which enabled me to heal the internal opposites that accompany black and white thinking: light and dark, masculine and feminine, believer and infidel, sacred and secular.

With mature spirituality, we can hold the tension of opposites, such as immanent and transcendent, and see the beauty in paradoxes, such as a human being who is wise and has a shadow. Paradoxical thinking—both/and—frees us from the self-righteousness of either/or thinking. And it can slowly release us from the need for certainty—and open us to the mystery of life.

Finally, we can learn or, in some cases, relearn how to define our own values and compose our own lives. The aim here is not, as cult deprogrammers suggest, merely to normalize those leaving spiritual communities; it's not to help disillusioned believers conform or adjust to conventional values. The result of that approach is regressive, and the student who views her years of involvement as "missing years" is often filled with regret. The teacher or group is now viewed as bad, and the family or society becomes good, which involves the opposite split during membership.

Instead, our aim is to integrate and move beyond our individual spiritual and group experiences in such a way that evolution continues. As the old spiritual persona with all of its attendant roles and values dies, a new life is born.

Reclaiming authentic feeling

Our spiritual personas keep us functioning in a narrow range of feeling, whether for the purpose of a practice or for the purpose of control by a spiritual authority. For instance, we may cut off sexuality because of a traditional fear of Hell or anger because we are afraid of our own impulses. Or we may shut down grief or fear because of the forced optimism of a new age community, whose members insist that we "create reality" through positive or negative thinking.

I can remember the moment when an old friend asked why I always had a silly smile on my face when life was so difficult. I had not known that I had adopted a contented grin. But, when she pointed it out, I began to realize how urgently I wanted to feel contentment, balance, and equilibrium. The grin masked the dis-owned, difficult feelings that had been banished during my many years as a med-itation teacher, even from me.

It can be frightening to explore forbidden feelings and to seek out emotional authenticity after years of subtly training ourselves only to feel in limited ways. Mark Matousek wrote about reclaiming his own authentic emotions in his mem-oir, *Sex, Death, Enlightenment.* As a young boy, he desperately needed an image of victorious manhood and, armoring against his feelings, became obsessed with the appearance of strength and triumph. When he turned to Buddhism, his hero simply changed clothes. The fruits of self-inquiry substituted for the ideals of fame and fortune. And he fell in love with the seeker-as-hero and with the spiri-tual life as a glorious quest for the grail.

But in 1994 his mother suffered a terrible death. His ex-lover was diagnosed with the HIV virus. And he panicked with the terror of his own mortality. The shock of his vullnerability and helplessness pierced his spiritual armor. His per-petual optimism failed him, he landed on his knees and, as he put it, without the ability to stand up tall he didn't know who he was.

As every doubt assailed him, so did doubt in the *dharma.* The results of his practice disappeared, leaving him feeling like a fraud. His spiritual life did not save him from suffering as "ignorant" people suffered. And he lost the pride that protected his fictitious hero-self from humiliation.

When Matousek faced his terror of weakness, the hero crumbled. As his for-bidden feelings flooded him—fear, disappointment, failure, negativity, iner-tia—he felt raw and exposed. Those very shadow qualities that he most despised in others he was forced to face in himself. At last, he wrote, he joined humanity in a new way, as a fragile, wandering soul, a real person in real distress, with no ulti-mate solution.

Matousek grieved as he buried his mother. He grieved for his ex-lover. He grieved for his own invulnerable hero-self. And he discovered, to his surprise, that grief was the antidote to his inflation and his feelings of separateness. And that long-lost feeling opened the door to another vision of spirit, which was stripped of ideals, grandiose images, superhuman power, and rapturous talk of enlighten-ment. He felt the pain and the relief of letting the spiritual hero die and becom-ing an authentic human being.

Reclaiming the body

In many religious traditions, the primary splitting of opposites takes place between flesh and spirit. As the argument goes, the body is the container of evil forces, and the devil resides in its instinctual, animal impulses. We (our conscious egos) must strive to control them at all costs, redirecting our desires for higher purposes.

This view of the human body is sacrosanct in patriarchal cultures, especially in celibate monastic traditions (Christian, Buddhist, Muslim, or Hindu), in which priests value only the "higher" realms of spirit, mind, and rational thought. And the "lower" realms of soul, body, and nonrational feeling are banished into shadow. And it has been reinforced by the Cartesian mind/body split that we inherit from science.

In *Beyond Religion*, David Elkins said that, when he was a minister, most spiritual problems among his male congregants were sexual problems. These men were not acting inappropriately but were suffering terribly with the "sin of lust." Because the church taught them that the feeling of lust was as sinful as the action of adultery, they struggled with guilt and shame, banishing any erotic thoughts or feelings into the shadow. And the women in the congregation were not permitted to wear shorts or other revealing clothing that might cause a man to have impure thoughts. These Christian women got the message that they were not to look too attractive because, if a man felt lust for them, they were equally responsible for the sin.

Given this cultural milieu, which is common in conservative Christian and Muslim communities, many of us learn at a young age to live outside our bodies, identifying with mind or spirit, and to devalue and over-control them. If as adults we adopt a new tradition with this body-negative message, it resonates with this early teaching. So, we are attracted to doctrines that devalue this world and the body and to spiritual practices that may lead to dissociation. The teachings may look different at first: a change of language, a change of clothes. But the diminishment of embodied life is the same.

When I first entered my meditation community, there was no public position about sexuality. In fact, it was purported to be a practice for "householders," or people who married and had careers. But after I became a teacher, I heard increasingly negative messages about sex: celibacy would speed enlightenment, devotees around the teacher must be celibate, and sexual energy was crude or "gross."

With my liberal upbringing and education I had never heard this kind of overt negative attitude about sexuality before. But I can see now that it resonated with covert childhood messages from my parents, which instilled fear, guilt, and shame about bodily feelings, as opposed to verbal messages, which were more liberal. As a result, the archaic Hindu teachings let me off the hook. With celibacy for a higher purpose, I no longer needed to deal with difficult bodily feelings.

In a strange twist, bodily repression may cause some of the exact behavior that it is meant to keep at bay, including rape and incest. When the body hardens against feeling and emotional vitality is damped, we attempt to become obedient, even docile. But our buried impulses build charge in the shadow and may erupt unpredictably, as we saw in the stories of priests and teachers.

Just as forbidden thoughts and feelings can be cues to enhance spiritual shadow-work, so can forbidden bodily sensations or symptoms. Our bodies register the subtlties of our experiences, even beneath our conscious awareness. So, they contain hidden information about risks and dangers, longings and desires. A woman told me that each time she had an audience with her Buddhist teacher, her mind felt calm, but her pulse raced, her hands sweated, and her body would not be still. At first, she attributed the bodily response to anxiety. Of course, she would be nervous under the gaze of this great meditation master.

But, months later, when the teacher tried to seduce one of her friends, she was shocked: her body had been trying to warn her of danger. She simply did not know how to listen to the wisdom of its language.

Perhaps the most surprising and disturbing insight I had, after leaving my community, was that my physical mortality had not been altered by decades of practice. Somehow, somewhere I had come to believe that, through meditation, I would attain a level of consciousness that would ward off death. This transformation of the human condition, I believed, was the inevitable end point of right practice. And yet, from the instant that I left the sangha, I knew that it was not true.

It took a long time, however, for me to accept the new realization. The profound disappointment that accompanied it threw me into despair. Like my fears of intimacy, sexuality, and failure, I would have to face my fear of death.

I began to wonder whether my longing for the light had been, after all, a flight from death. A flight from darkness, doubt, intimacy, even responsibility, yes. But a flight from death?

Perhaps, beneath all the other fears, the fear of death lurked in me as it does in so many others. But instead of building castles of money, power, or fame to ensure my immortality, I built a castle of spirit.

Reclaiming action on our own behalf

A primary purpose of religion is to set the world of darkness or shadow against the world of light. To help ensure that its members participate in the light and avoid the dark, each tradition prescribes certain behaviors and proscribes others, slicing the possibilities for human action into good and evil. In such a black-and-white universe, right and wrong are two distinct paths, one leading to heaven, salvation, or enlightenment, the other to hell.

If we believe in this promise of salvation, project the *imago dei* onto a religious guide, and sacrifice our independent thinking and authentic feeling, then we will probably also sacrifice our agency, our capacity to take initiative on our own behalf—especially if that initiative involves disobeying a religious authority who exerts overt or covert control over our membership and, therefore, over our salvation.

In his twenties, a client joined a small group led by a kundalini yoga teacher, whose charisma and knowledge attracted intelligent students. My client was drawn to the promise of spiritual awakening through secret practices, which quickly opened his psychic abilities, leading him to revere the teacher. When the older man forbid his students from eating meat, engaging in sexual relationships and masturbation, and wearing gems or jewels of any kind, my client acquiesced.

"It all made sense in the context of working with energies," he told me. "We sought to refine our energies and transform them from the grosser to the subtler by sending them up the spine to generate kundalini."

At a more covert level, he said, the teacher forbid the seeking of power of any kind and the expression of ego in the forms of individual desire or passion. Again, my client tried to obey. He directed his ambition toward spiritual attainments. Eventually, he felt no passion for anything but enlightenment.

But one night the teacher tested my client's ability to obey: he told the student to kneel and give him oral sex. As a kundalini adept, the teacher said, he would transform the sexual energy generated by this act into spiritual energy for both men. My client submitted.

But from that moment he was tormented by doubt and filled with shame. His teacher was a hypocrite, who preached celibacy and engaged in a secret sex life. My client's obedience to the teacher's moral values suddenly seemed wrong, even sinful. His devotion, a source of such sweetness, turned sour. The meditation practices, previously so alluring, became unappealing.

Yet, for weeks, he could not take action. He sat, passively, unable to speak up or act on his own behalf. He walked about in a daze, unable to eat or sleep. He faced a terrible crisis: was he more commited to this man than to his own well being? Should he continue to obey this man rather than make his own decisions?

As he lost weight and suffered from insomnia, he sought out medical advice from a trusted healer. This man told him he needed to eat meat and deal with his sexual energy. But if my client listened to the healer's advice, he would have to disobey his teacher. Slowly and gradually, he came to the conclusion that, at this stage of his spiritual life, obedience to this spiritual authority was no longer healthy for him. Disobedience was required for his evolution. He left the group.

As a result, he began to date women, explore sexuality, and think about a career, all of which had been forbidden to him. At first he simply rebelled, eager to experiment with every taboo. But gradually he established his own internal moral compass.

Taking courses in the field of psychology, he learned about Kohlberg's stages of moral develoment. In the first stage, he told me, "I was obedient to avoid punishment. Then I became identified with being the good disciple, and my compliance was based on the teacher's approval. Finally, I'm learning how to act morally because it fits my own moral values. With the help of psychotherapy, I'm now internalizing my own spiritual authority."

I have heard stories like this man's from members of every tradition. For example, teachers who suggest that prayer, meditation, or scripture alone can solve practical problems cultivate passivity in their followers. When a problem remains intransient, believers blame themselves because they cannot blame god or their teacher. Reclaiming action on own behalf, we can reverse this passivity, not merely to react or rebel in an adolescent way, but to act from adult conscious choice.

Furthermore, we can reclaim our power to act on behalf of others. In addition to believing that spirituality was only "up," many of us also came to think that it was only directed "in." That is, a movement "out" into the world was not a spiritual move, but a political one. Today we need to heal the split between "in" and "out," introverted spiritual practice and extroverted social action.

We need to bring those qualities that we have developed through contemplative practice back to humanity to serve others in need and to change the institutions that perpetrate abuse and oppression. This is not a call for social action that stems from unconscious projection—"We are the people and they are the enemy." It's not a call for action that stems from a patronizing superiority—"They are downtrodden and we can save them." It is a call for action that stems from the awareness of our common humanity, the knowledge that each of us yearns for something greater, and the wisdom that the shadow lurks around the corner.

Reclaiming images of the divine

When the human spirit has come of age, it cannot return to the image of god as a heavenly parent.

—Bishop John Spong

The ecstatic lover has burning faith in every divine manifestation—as formless radiance, as various forms or attributes, as divine incarnations like Rama and Krishna, and as the goddess of wisdom, who is beyond form and formlessness, containing both in her mystic womb.

—Ramakrishna

Finally, we need to reimagine the *imago* and reclaim personal images of god that lie at the root of so much suffering. If our images of the divine do not fit our gender, temperament, ethnicity, or stage of life, they may no longer serve as divine guides but act, instead, as shadow figures by sabotaging our spiritual intentions. We can learn to reimagine them so that we are, indeed, made in the image of our god. As a result, we can begin to distinguish the voice of the divine, in answer to our prayers, from the chorus of inner voices that keeps us from quietude.

In a 1983 U.S. survey, nearly 1600 people scored the following images of god: Judge, King, Lover, Master, Father, Redeemer, Friend, Healer, Mother, Liberator, Spouse, and Creator. The last, Creator, was the dominant image for 82 per cent of the people. Spouse was the least popular at 17 per cent. Twenty-five per cent imagined god as Mother, especially older persons. In addition, in the survey women embraced the images more than men. And educated people were less likely to accept any of them.

But these statistics do not reflect the reality of the religious unconscious at all periods of human history. The late Jungian analyst Ed Edinger described the stages of evolution of the god image in Western civilization: in animism, the individual is embedded in an environment filled with spirits. In matriarchy, the earth mother is at the center of fertility rites, death and rebirth cycles tied to the land. With the rise of cities in Mesopotamia, Egypt, and Greece, polytheism emerged with its family of deities that were headed by a father, much like the city's king. Among the Hebrews, tribal monotheism arose and with it the possibility of a personal relationship to god, who ruled by the law. A more universal monotheism emerged with Christianity, including the images of the good son, Jesus, and the bad son, Lucifer.

Finally, with Kant, the god image leapt into the interior world. Jung pointed out that, since Kant, we must recognize that all of our experience is filtered through our subjectivity. We cannot experience a god or an archetype directly; we can only experience its effects via our own psyches. Jung referred to this as the reality of the psyche.

Once we see through our subjective filters, we no longer identify with a single image of god, Edinger said. We see it as a living reality in our own souls. And each experience of it—each meeting with an overwhelming archetype—is a defeat for the ego. This is the path of individuation, the current stage of evolution of the god image for Jungians.

This perceptual shift has dramatic consequences for our religious traditions. If we make this distinction between inner or subjective reality and outer factors, then we may begin to favor an internal rather than an external image of god. So, for example, in Judaism, the sacred object of longing is the Messiah, who will usher in the return of paradise and the end of the separation between the human lover and the divine beloved. Is the Messiah to be thought of as a human being who will appear, like the prophets, on the world scene? Or is it to be imagined as our own Messiah nature, which lives in all human souls?

The latter is the radical stance taken by Hasids, or mystical Jews, who believe that the secret, inner Messiah nature sleeps within all living beings—and has awakened in their illumined teachers, or *tzaddiks*. The eighteenth-century founder of Hasidism, the Bal Sham Tov, whose name means master of the names of god, danced with ecstatic abandon to fuel the fires of his longing for union. He was so filled with divine presence as he sang and danced that his individual ego dissolved in transcendence, just as whirling dervishes dissolve in *fana*.

The same dilemma appears in traditional vs. mystical Christianity. Is Jesus the one and only Christ? Or is the Christ nature hidden beneath our human nature in every one of us?

A medieval Christian monk, Thomas a Kempis, wrote a guide for the faithful that advocates the practices of humility, charity, and obedience. He urged believers to turn toward the will of god through prayer and scripture and away from materialism, willfulness, and pride. His model for this pious life was Jesus, as evidenced in the name of his book: *imitatio* Christ.

The monk took Christ's words—"He who follows me walks not in darkness"—to mean that Christians needed to imitate Jesus's life and manners. Stories abound of saints and seekers who have strived to live as Christ lived: to feed the hungry, to suffer as the crucified Christ, to be reborn as he was resurrected. The fourteenth-century anchoress Julian of Norwich asked three things of god: to experience the suffering of those who witnessed Christ's passion; to experience a severe illness at age thirty that mirrored his pain and terror of death; and to experience the wounds of contrition and compassion, and the wound of longing with her will for god.

In this century in Italy, Padre Pio yearned to be purified of his sins and therefore embraced the suffering Christ. For thirty years he manifested continuously the five wounds or stigmata of Christ. During mass, he claimed to be united with Jesus, like two candles burning into one, and to relive the Christian drama. Some observers saw a crown of thorns on his brow. After mass, witnesses wiped blood from his head and clothes.

In the twelfth century, the Christian god looked like a king or judge, and people behaved toward him as toward their feudal lord. But, when a new god image arose in human consciousness—god as beloved—a more devotional feeling spread among both male and female aspirants. As a result, spousal mysticism emerged, in which monks and nuns anointed themselves to prepare for the kiss of Christ, the experience of union with him.

Saint Clare of Assisi, whose unconsummated love for St. Francis is legendary, was bound in her soul to Christ. Living with absolute poverty, she freed herself of personal desires and worked to serve and heal those in need. She understood the inner workings of the *imago dei* when she wrote: "Place your heart in the figure of the divine substance. And transform your entire being into the image of the godhead itself through contemplation."

A contemporary woman described for me her passion for Christ. In the tradition of St. Teresa of Avila, who sang, danced, and played tamborine as she ardently burned for her beloved Jesus, this woman also called herself a bride of Christ. A divorce lawyer by day, she had a secret life at night. I asked her to write the story of that part of herself:

> As the darkness falls, the longing rises. As the sun sets below the horizon, and the container turns from blue to black, I turn from a woman of day to a woman of night. I become a bride of Christ.
>
> I remove the colors that adorn me, the shades of gold that complement my hair, the shades of blue that bring out my eyes. I remove the watch that keeps me prompt and the jewels on my ears that join me to tribal women the world over. For at night I wear white, nothing more. And I stand alone, not as part of any lineage.

Slowly, I purify my body, cleansing it of ambition and fear, smoothing it of sharp edges and jagged points. The chores of the day are lifted from my muscles and then the deeper burdens, the heavier cares wash away. As my body lightens, it becomes an instrument for His symphony. It is tuned to His tune. It plays only His song.

I cleanse my mind, emptying it of human images, of people hungry and lost, of people wanting, wanting. I open my mind as the shore opens to the sea, by simple being there, in the way of the sea. And the waves rush in, unceasingly. Then my mind can wait, wait without hope, for Him to arrive.

As my body is washed clean as a bone dried in the desert sun, and my mind is as empty as the simple tone of a gong, I open to receive Him. I open like a new bride to her groom. And the smallest residue that remained in me of the day is pushed aside as He enters me slowly and fills me fully. And I know once again why I am a bride of Christ.

Jung, who wrote extensively about this tradition, believed that in general the goal of *imitatio* Christ—behave like Christ and become like him—has not been fulfilled. Jesus, he said, has been turned into an external object of worship, a concrete icon, which prevents it from sinking down into the depths of the soul, as the teaching intended. That is, discipleship has become imitation; symbol has become idol.

Pious believers use Christ's image as a way to escape doing their own spiritual work. As Jung put it, Christ lived his own unique life regardless of convention and as a heretic in his own tradition. He took up his own cross, his own destiny, as we need to take up ours. But, instead, we believe that Christ and his cross can deliver us from our conflicts. Instead of bearing the tension of our own opposites and walking through our own darkness, we ask him to carry our burdens and remain as children in relation to an all-powerful Other.

This concrete rather than symbolic use of an *imago* can take place in any tradition. Some followers of Eastern teachers also mimic their behavior or phraseology, their diet or dress. They place the teachers outside themselves as divine mediators, rather than assimilating them internally as images of the Self. There may be stages in which it is helpful for an outer figure (guru, priest, or therapist) to carry a projection of the Self for awhile, if at some point the seeker recognizes it, struggles with it, and eventually sees that it belongs in her own treasury. But, if she adores the teacher indefinitely, the process is thwarted. The believer remains untouched in the deepest parts of herself and stuck in a projection of the Self.

Cultural shifts reflect shifting images of god even today. Leaders of the mytho-poetic men's movement pointed out years ago that many boys in our culture suffer from a "father wound," the absence of an older man who can affirm their masculinity. Certainly, some boys and men with this unmet need yearn to find someone to fill it, such as a surrogate father or a father-god.

Certain Christian groups that advocate sonship in relation to Jesus can fill this gap for believers. As Gordon Dalbey put it, "Who can a man go to in order to get what he missed from Dad? When a man realizes that no human being can meet his need, he's ready to get real and cry out for his true Father God." His ministry invites men to bring their wounds to Jesus, where two or three are gathered in His name.

Other Christians have vocally critiqued their tradition from within, calling for believers to re-imagine the images of the son, the father, and the mother of god. In *Why Christianity Must Change or Die*, Anglican Bishop John Spong pointed out that the hunger for god is deep and pervasive, but it's not the same as the hunger for answers that the church traditionally gives. It's the Christian task, he said, to return to the direct experience that led to church creeds.

Spong has called himself a believer in exile: he is committed to Jesus Christ, but he is exiled from literal understandings of Christianity, including archaic images of god. In a radical leap away from the church, he suggested that, given the discoveries of science and psychology, a theistic personal god with parental or supernatural qualities—a divine worker of miracles, a dispenser of rewards and punishments—has become outdated.

In particular, Spong selected the image of Jesus as rescuer for re-imagining. Jesus was cast in the role because of our need to overcome the fall in the Garden of Eden and to restore the world to the perfection intended by god, Spong said. Jesus came "down," became the perfect sacrifice, and removed the consequences of sin in the crucifixion. With the resurrection, he traveled "up," and in this way god validated his offering.

Spong sees through this narrative with the aid of the theory of evolution. The fall becomes, for him, the dawn of self-consciousness. Similarly, with the aid of the cycle of consciousness described earlier, we can imagine that each of us "falls" from unconscious union and travels "down" into incarnation until we consciously begin to yearn for union once again. Jesus can become, as Spong calls him, a spirit person, a window onto the holy, and an image of what each of us might look like in a fully realized state.

A friend of mine always remembered a stained glass window in her childhood church, which portrayed an image of Jesus praying in the garden before his death. Beneath the image were the words: "Not my will but thine be done."

She told me that this image set her on her path. It would reappear for years later in her prayers. And she would recall it at moments when she cried out to god.

In her fifties, she returned to her childhood church, accompanied by her mother. They found that the window had been taken down. But after some investigation they discovered it in the church basement. With help, they pulled it out and set it up so that the sun lit it from behind. My friend sobbed as she stood and reclaimed her original *imago dei*.

In *Avalanche*, Brugh Joy told a similar tale of a woman at a conference. Deeply involved in Buddhism, this woman resented her early Christian upbringing. Sitting in a morning meditation with the aim of allowing images of rise up out of her unconscious, she was shocked when an angel appeared, announcing that her name was Veronica. The woman told Brugh, "I don't believe in angels. Too Christian."

A few days later, the woman was meditating—and Christ appeared. In her imagery, she ran from him, upset that a Christian figure was desecrating her sacred place. But moments later Veronica appeared and reassured her that Christ and his teachings were part of her future evolution. Her defenses dropped, and she allowed this disowned *imago* to return to the sacred for her.

Other women have turned toward feminine images of the divine after failing to find adequate reflection in masculine images. As Julian of Norwich said, "God is the true Father and Mother of nature. God almighty is our loving father, and god all wisdom is our loving mother."

In the same way that we, as children, develop a sense of self in relation to a mother who is present, comforting, and containing, and whom we can idealize, so some of us develop a larger sense of trust in life in relation to a divine mother. We long for an image of the divine feminine that is accepting, consoling, and healing. While women have explored feminine spirituality to find a god who looks like them, some men, like several male clients of mine, yearn for god as mother, declaring that only from her do they feel unconditional acceptance.

During the Paleolithic and Neolithic eras, the goddess spun the web of life. She was seen in ancient stone, rhythmic oceans, and womb-like eggs. She was honored in undulating snakes, ageless trees, and the sweet-scented rose. In ancient Greece, Gaia, mother of the gods and the earth, and her daughter Demeter, goddess of the grains, maintained a link to the Neolithic great mother, before the rise of the patriarchal age and the rule of Zeus.

In ancient Egypt, the goddess Maat, an ostrich feather on her head, personified divine harmony and balance. Isis, wife of Osiris, was worshipped for three thousand years as queen of heaven, queen of earth, and queen of the underworld. Hathor, the divine cow mother, needed only to imagine a thing for it to manifest. She was worshipped as the star Sirius, and her devotees sang and danced in her temple. In her form as Sekhmet, the lion-headed goddess with a musical rattle and healing necklace, she could bring destruction by withholding the waters of life.

A friend told me that most of the women in her family had taken action but remained invisible. They were afraid to reveal themselves. She wanted to know her own innate power; she desired to feel her anger at its root. She made a pilgrimage to the Temple of Karnak in Egypt to see the seven-foot black statue of Sekhmet, the lion-headed goddess.

In a dark chamber, my friend sang and chanted to the goddess in high, intense bursts of sound that surprised even her. The goddess's eyes, a flat paint in one moment, suddenly sparkled to life and shone love on my friend. Not a soft, gentle love, but love and power, she said. Sekhmet embodied ferociousness, a raw force. But my friend called it the heart of power—strength and compassion. Following this ritual moment, she was no longer afraid of her own inner resources; she was no longer ashamed of her power. She broke the pattern of her female lineage.

A lovely client in her thirties told me that she felt unattractive and, although she loved her husband deeply, she had no interest in sex. For a long time, she insisted that her parents had given her an ideal childhood and had the kind of marriage that she wished to emulate.

Slowly, during the course of our work together, she gained a more complex view of them, which included their shadows and limitations. Struggling with her dislike and shame about them, she began to explore her own womanhood. Her matronly and self-sacrificing mother had offered no model of healthy femininity. So, instead, she had identified with her charismatic, workaholic father who, she said, never related to her femininity. As an adult, she had rejected the Christian church of her childhood and replaced it with a "rational need to understand," which she viewed as a more adult relation to god.

In her leisure time, she began to visit museums for inspiration and renewal. Sitting one day across from a painting of Aphrodite, she suddenly felt worshipful.

She discovered in that moment that she faced an image of the divine that was her, yet not her.

As she sat with the image, her mind quieted, her breath slowed. She felt a deep sense of recognition in that moment, a self-recognition that had been lying just beneath the boundaries of awareness. She loved this goddess just as she was—and wanted only to remain in her presence. She felt no need to do anything, to be anywhere. She wanted only this timeless moment with her.

"This is what religion should be," she told me.

In her journal, she began a dialogue with Aphrodite, who was surprisingly talkative. And eventually the woman found clues to her own feminine beauty and passion reflected in the goddess.

The widespread need for non-white images of the divine arises naturally from the racial and ethnic diversity of our culture. Today there are more than 12 million people of Mexican descent in the U.S., and the divine mother, in the form of Our Lady of Guadalupe, is one of their principle images of god. When Cortez and the Spaniards invaded Mexico in the sixteenth century and slaughtered millions of native Indians in the name of Jesus, a miracle occurred in Mexico City. While walking to church, a peasant heard celestial music and a heavenly lady appeared, cloaked by the sun. Calling him "the smallest and most beloved of my children," she told the man that she was the mother of god, mother of the creator. And she wanted a temple built for her on the nearby site of an Aztec shrine.

The bishop responded to the peasant's request by asking for a sign from the Lady. First, she cured the man's uncle, who was terminally ill. Next, she sent him to find out-of-season roses, which he arranged in his cloak. Standing before the bishop, he opened the cloak and the flowers scattered on the ground. The three-dimensional image of the Lady was imprinted on the cloak in bright colors.

A client, who is part-Catholic Latina, part-Jewish, had always hidden her ethnic identity. Her parents had kept their mixed racial and religious past a secret and asked her to do the same. As a result, she felt unseen, unknown, and fraudulent. While openly exploring her Latino lineage in therapy for the first time, she felt compelled to make a journey to the cathedral in Mexico City where the image of the Lady of Guadalupe is enshrined.

Standing before her, my client felt awe. She was moved by the sunlight emanating from her, the stars on her cloak, the moon beneath her feet, and the angel who holds her up on the moon. But, mostly, she felt stunned by the eyes, which look alive because they reflect images of other people who appear to be in front of her.

For the first time, this woman saw an image of the divine who also seemed to see her, all of her, the real her. In the Lady's mirror reflection, this woman felt less alone and more authentic than she had ever felt. As a result, she began to reclaim the neglected part of her cultural and spiritual heritage, which had been hidden in the family shadow.

Although this woman's encounter with a god image was shaped by an emotional unmet need, it cannot be explained by that alone. She beheld an *imago dei*, a powerful and mysterious Other that transcended her ego awareness. And it, in turn, beheld her.

Some African-Americans also yearn for god-images that look like them. In an unpublished study, psychologist Rossalyn Marie Richardson tied white images of god and biblical characters to low self-esteem in Christian blacks. Cultural pride has been low, she pointed out, because blacks have attempted to live with a false cultural self, which is rooted in idealizing a wrong racial *imago*.

She pointed out that during slavery white masters seemed all-powerful and god-like to African slaves. Blacks wanted the approval of their white masters, she said, and they internalized a view of themselves as inferior. When they then imagined Biblical images, they visualized them as white and superior.

According to participants in Richardson's study, black males exposed early in life to Biblical characters as black had higher self-esteem. Although several participants claimed that the racial identity of the Bible's characters was irrelevant to them, one African American man reported that his relationship to god improved after he discovered that the historical Jesus could have been black, based on one theory of geneology.

Creativity as practice

I suggest that a daily spiritual life can be more authentic when it is rooted in the yearning of the human soul. Our particular form of holy longing can offer a glimpse into the hidden object of our desire. And it, in turn, can lead us backward to self-knowledge and forward to our destiny.

Rather than training us to value only certain aspects of life and to devalue others, our spirituality can help us to reclaim "down" and to proclaim "up." Instead of insisting that we blindly accept received knowledge and pre-existing *imagoes*, it can help us to fertilize our imaginations, to dream of new possibilities in art and culture and even in our social systems, which cry out for radical reform. To do this, religious and spiritual institutions would need to include and honor what Matthew Fox called the Via Creativa.

In *Original Blessing*, Fox suggested that when we allow ourselves to fully experience the Via Positiva, the way of light and blessings, as well as the Via Negativa, the way of darkness and shadow, we come to know creation and the void, fullness and emptiness. Out of their union, a third thing emerges: the word or image—signaling the birth of new creation.

In the creative moment we are, as Meister Eckhart said, generative as god is. We are like the creator and, therefore, living in its image. That is, the *imago dei* is no longer outside us; it is in us, in the soul, in the imagination, creating new life. In the Christian mythos, this is the resurrection.

Of course, it may not mean that we have attained higher levels of union, such as psychic, subtle, or causal levels, which may be attained by Rumi, St. Catherine, and Ramakrishna, among others. But it can mean that the internalized *imago* fuels creative work, directing our longing toward new images and new work.

On the other hand, when the holy longing is twisted or denied, the forces of creation turn destructive. Misplaced creativity can lead to a drive for power in which the human energies of innovation and ingenuity are harnessed for destruction, as we long to vanquish an enemy or prove that god is on our side.

In effect, the life of the imagination *is* the spiritual life. We must, as Rainer Maria Rilke put it, give birth to our images. "They are the future waiting to be born."

Many years ago, as a new meditator, I believed that sitting practice alone was a spiritual act; meditation alone constituted a spiritual life. My reasoning: only meditation sent my energy and attention up.

Therefore, a clear line was drawn for me between sacred and profane activities. But my sacred wound of disillusionment also led to the discovery of writing as a spiritual practice, which opened my imagination in magical, unexpected ways.

I never dreamed of becoming a author. I didn't fantasize about writing the great American novel or winning a Pulitzer for investigative journalism. But, in 1981, after leaving my spiritual community, I met a writer who had just published a groundbreaking bestseller. We felt an immediate kinship. Although I had no writing experience, she hired me to be the editor of her publications, which explored innovations in consciousness research.

I vividly recall the first day on the job: I sat at the terminal, blank mind facing blank screen—paralyzed. But as I began to take assignments, become engaged with research, and articulate exciting ideas, I found that journalism fit my temperament: I fully enjoyed gathering information, seemed to have a gift for synthesizing it, and thrilled to the thought of transmitting it to others.

Then I submitted it to my editor. She took a red pencil and deleted or altered every word. The text returned to me unrecognizable. My heart sank. She demanded a dense and telegraphed style in order to jam data into a small space. But it could not remain abstract and remote; the verbs needed to carry it off the page. And it could not show a trace of me; in the objective voice, the subject disappears.

As a novice, I was eager to learn. So, I submitted and rewrote ... and rewrote ... and rewrote. Finally, an article was accepted. And the process began again on the next piece. I heavily researched a topic; synthesized various sources; quoted a range of points of view; uncovered a key conclusion. And she marked it up in bright red.

One evening, at the terminal for a typical ten-hour day, tears running down my cheeks, I was about to give up. I felt hopeless: I would never become a journalist and certainly would never please this woman. And yet ... I had felt such joy in finding just the right word to make a sentence fly. I had felt such gratification in hearing from satisfied readers.

Suddenly, I remembered a story from the Tibetan Buddhist tradition: a solitary monk named Milarepa lived in the woods on nettle soup and practiced meditation day and night. For many years he tried to attain realization, but his fasting and prayers were not enough. One day another man, Marpa, emerged from the woods and their eyes met: Milarepa felt an instant bond and recognized Marpa as his teacher.

Marpa asked him to build a small stone house in a certain corner of the woods, "over there," then disappeared among the trees. For the next year, Milarepa gathered stones, one by one, lifted them slowly, and carried them to the site. Then with painstaking attention he fit them together until they formed a sturdy structure.

Marpa emerged from the woods, glanced at the stone house, turned his back on it and, pointing in another direction, said, "Oh, no, over there!" Then he wandered off into the forest.

Milarepa's heart sank. But he set about his task as if he had no choice. He began to take apart the house stone by stone, carry each one to the other site, lift it, and fit it into place. A year later, he stood back and viewed the house with a sense of satisfaction at completing the task.

Just then, Marpa returned, approached the house, shook his head, and proclaimed, "Oh, no, over there!" as he pointed in a third direction.

Again, Milarepa submitted. Again, he took apart what he had built and carried the stones to the new area. Again he fit them together until the house stood once more. And again Marpa appeared, shook his head and pointed "No, over there."

After Milarepa rebuilt the house that time, the story goes, he became enlightened.

I stared at the terminal, tears dried, smiling. I had believed that only my meditation was spiritual practice. But clearly the work of writing and rewriting could also teach me about unattachment, impermanence, and discrimination.

I began to write as if setting words in a sentence were setting stones in a house. I wrote as if my awareness of the writing process were more important than the content of the writing. To my surprise, I saw fewer red marks; the writing got better!

Soon I discovered another key: I would do intensive research, then sit down to meditate for an hour, emptying my mind, relaxing my body, letting go completely of the writing project. When I returned to the empty screen, words flowed from me in an easy river, no struggle. Slowly, I learned to trust this process: filling the mind, emptying the mind, getting out of the way. And the red marks disappeared.

The cycle of mentoring was over. But the writing life had just begun. And my spiritual journey continued, as it included wider and wider orbits of life.

A spiritually authentic life is an ongoing creative act, in which the creature and the creator long to be united. If we choose to live it within an existing tradition, a finished work of art, we can decorate it with our own detail. If we choose to live it outside of tradition, we can design it with images from our own soul.

Finding our spiritual myths

Myth is the secret opening through which the inexhaustible energies of the cosmos pour into human cultural manifestation.

—Joseph Campbell

As I wrote in the book's opening, a psychological lens is necessary in order to extend our model of spirituality; it's necessary in order to recover from spiritual abuse and disillusionment. But it's not sufficient. At this point, we can lift off the lens of psychology and view our spiritual journeys through the lens of myth.

In this way, we can see beyond our personal, local histories to the universal patterns that lie beneath them or behind them. In these timeless larger stories, we are the heroes and the princesses, the wanderers and the warriors, the healers and the saints.

Like us, the protagonists of myth begin life in innocence, their awareness limited to their immediate environment. Unexpectedly, they hear a call to adventure, an invitation to leave home to find Home. Reluctant to change or risk danger, a few refuse the call.

But if they meet a key person, such as a potential partner or beloved teacher, they overcome their reluctance and cross a threshold: they leave the familiar, conventional world of family, friends, childhood beliefs and values. They follow their holy longing and find that it leads them away from the known toward something more, something mysterious or transcendent. This departure signifies the first stage of any rite of passage: separation.

In early experiments with the new life, the hero undergoes tests, such as those exacted by a new romantic relationship or a religious teacher. These trials may test the hero's loyalty, obedience, compassion, or level of self-knowledge. The hero may find allies while meeting these challenges and may encounter enemies, who attempt to get him or her to resist change or to alter direction.

Eventually, the hero faces a primary ordeal: the encounter with the shadow in the form of a beast, a whale, a minotaur, a dragon. Similarly, during the ordeal of a loving partnership, the hero meets the shadow of her idealized beloved—a cold, cruel, or unconscious aspect of the beloved's nature. Likewise, in a spiritual discipleship, he or she meets an idealized teacher's greed, self-centeredness, or hunger for power.

In myth, the dark side of the gods is evident: Hermes, the trickster, lies and steals. Hades abducts and violates Persephone. Theseus abandons Ariadne. Even in the Bible, Abraham exiles his son, Ishmael, Judas betrays Jesus, and Joseph is banished by his father and brothers. Those who are wounded suffer in real ways.

In another context, the ordeal may take the form of an illness, an accident, or a loss that awakens the hero to her mortality. But in every case, the hero's innocence is lost. This encounter signifies the second stage of a rite of passage: descent and initiation.

In facing the ordeal, we may at first succumb to denial and attempt to hide from the new awareness. We cannot bear to see our ideal tarnished, mortal. Instead of consciously following the descent, we stop—and fall helplessly into depression, going down without undergoing initiation.

At this time, we may feel forsaken by loved ones, allies, even god. Just as one who struggles with addiction may need to reach bottom before feeling the touch of a higher power, we may need to feel that all is lost—before Spirit is found.

But if the hero is to complete the journey, this setback is only temporary. A renewed attempt to deal with the shadow arises.

And beneath the concrete violation a hidden alchemical process takes place. When we follow each of the mythic stories above to its conclusion, the moment of descent is also a moment of awakening. Persephone, once an innocent mother's girl, becomes queen of the underworld, able to hold both darkness and light. The abandoned Ariadne is led to marry a god, Dionysus, becoming immortal. Joseph becomes counselor to the pharaoh and a wise interpreter of dreams. Jesus, betrayed, is led to his crucifixion and, ultimately, to his resurrection.

So, if this rite is sacralized, and the concrete process becomes alchemical, disillusionment becomes dissolution. We surrender the ego's control and that which appeared to be solid and unchanging—our beliefs, opinions, attachments, fears—liquefies. Suddenly, we see through it.

The idealized teacher, whom we thought we could not live without, becomes another vulnerable human being, no matter how spiritually adept. The dogma we gripped to ward off meaninglessness becomes another series of words, perhaps of value, perhaps not. The fear of loss of community, of religious loneliness, becomes the doorway to courage, to a more authentic life.

This has been my experience again and again: at the bottom of a descent, my mind, its precious concepts, its need to be right, its rejection of what is—all dissolve, and my sense of self explodes. Inevitably, my heart opens to include more and more.

And the ascent begins again. I transcend to the next level of awareness, all the while including everything that has come before. And I step onto the other shore.

From there the hero looks back and sees how innocent she was, how blind, how narrow-minded. And, with this new level of awareness, she can never go back again. She can honor both the concrete violation that stems from meeting the shadow, including the painful feelings that it evokes, and its mythic meaning, which sets the suffering in the larger story. And she can see how evolution itself is as work in her life.

Transformed, the hero enters the third stage—the return. He or she follows the road back to the world with a boon: the sword, the stone, the new level of consciousness. For Rumi, the gift of ecstatic poems of union with the Beloved. For Ramakrishna, the teachings of the great Advaita Vedanta. For Catherine of Siena, the modeling of a life joined to Christ. For me, this book.

A New Epilogue: Through the Shadow to the Light

Soon after the first publication of this book, in which I disclosed my deep disillusionment with the dream of awakening and my grief about not having met ordinary people who had fulfilled that dream, my life took a sharp right turn—and there they were: a few dozen men and women who, like me, had been dedicated to meditation for decades but who, unlike me, had passed through the advanced stages of awakening and now live full-time in non-duality or unitive consciousness. They would not call themselves heroes, but they have completed the hero's journey, the great return of consciousness to its source.

During the past few years, I have come to know them well. Sitting in weekly *satsangs*, I have listened to the details of their original awakenings and of their ongoing moment-to-moment spiritual experiences. And I have been startled to discover the lived reality of enlightenment in all its splendor—and all its ordinariness.

My awakened friends appear in various shapes and sizes, with distinct temperaments and styles, and work as artists, business people, musicians, office workers—but they have no interest in being spiritual teachers. However, as friends, they have taught me much and reignited my inspiration and holy longing for enlightenment, which no longer seems like an unattainable dream.

I am currently at work on a new book about one such ordinary, extraordinary man, whose lived reality, which seems so natural to him, will startle any reader. So I will not describe this phenomenon at length here. Let me simply begin to give you a flavor of what I have learned.

The evolution of stages or levels of consciousness (as described above) does take place during awakening but not in the neat, orderly way I had imagined. For some individuals, a particular level may last for only a brief time. For instance, the witness or cosmic consciousness in one friend passed quickly, while for another it has endured for many years. In the latter's case, it has been a liberating but not so pleasant experience, accompanied by the freedom of less attachment to thoughts, feelings, and actions but the absence of bliss, love, or new knowledge. I was startled to hear him repeat again and again that he wished this stage would pass.

Also, the levels of consciousness may appear to be overlapping or simultaneous. For one friend, glimpses of deities or celestial realms (the divine mother, in his case) overlapped with glimpses of identification with Spirit. Although neither one has stabilized, he experiences both regularly.

A female friend evolved in a few months from the witness of cosmic consciousness, to experiences of deity mysticism or celestial perception, to experiences of identification with Spirit, to experiences of union with Spirit (*nirvakalpa samadhi*), to experiences of returning to the world of form and identifying all form as Spirit (*sahaj samadhi*). This level of complete non-duality is not conceptual for her; it's a direct experience. As she put it, the whole cosmos, far and near, is in her body. There is no more far and near, no self/other, no subject/object, no separation of any kind.

One startling finding: Many of these people have not completed their ego-homework and shadow-work. One woman, clearly awake, still struggles with very difficult emotional relationship issues. Another, an abuse survivor, still dissociates at odd moments, although she is aware of it. And one man still suffers compulsions, although he witnesses them.

So, I must conclude that they did not travel the linear path from pre-personal to personal (ego) to transpersonal work. Rather, they woke up in the spiritual line of development—and traces of their ignorance remained in their emotional and cognitive development. Each of them urged me to resolve emotional and shadow issues as much as possible before awakening so that the bliss and clarity of the higher level of consciousness can be fully appreciated.

In addition, they make a distinction between pain and suffering. One man, who was living at the level of *sahaj samadhi,* had a near-fatal car accident and lives with chronic back pain. However, he insists that he does not suffer. The pain is; the suffering is a choice.

We have had extensive discussions about the fate of the ego in evolution, the reality or unreality of free will, the emergence of special powers, the role of kundalini, and the true nature of death. These themes will be explored in my next book, not conceptually but in the direct experience of the awakened mind.

Today, among the *satsang* members, my dreams of transcendence and union are reborn. My faith is rekindled in holy longing, the impulse of evolution itself.

Having undergone the meeting with spiritual shadow and suffered the loss of innocence, which initiated me into the complexity of human life, I have found the narrow path through the darkness and find myself traveling again toward the light, toward a conscious reunion with the source, the Spirit, which already always is who I am.

978-0-595-44910-1
0-595-44910-7

LaVergne, TN USA
14 October 2009
160898LV00001B/152/P